THE BEAUTY OF LIGHT

Etel Adnan & Laure Adler

THE BEAUTY OF LIGHT:
INTERVIEWS WITH ETEL ADNAN

TRANSLATED BY ETHAN MITCHELL

Nightboat Books
New York

These conversations include, in the first two chapters, statements made during radio interviews of EA with LA on France Culture (2015) and on France Inter (2019).

France Culture, *Hors-champs,* 2015. © Radio France
France Inter, *L'Heure bleue*, 2019. © Radio France

This work was awarded the Albertine Translation Prize in fiction/non-fiction for excellence in publication and translation as part of Albertine Translation, a program created by Villa Albertine and funded by FACE Foundation and the Albertine Books Foundation with the support of Van Cleef & Arpels.

ISBN: 978-1-64362-211-8

Cover design and interior typesetting by Kit Schluter
Typeset in Garamond Premier Pro

Cataloging-in-publication data is available from the Library of Congress

Nightboat Books
New York
www.nightboat.org

Friendship

She said that driving a big car on a highway crossing the American desert was like doing calligraphy in her notebooks. She said that if you look at a mountain carefully and faithfully each day, you can become its friend. And this is what happened to her. Each thing that existed in the world provoked her curiosity, and often her wonder. She was never weary and always alert, as if to be alive were in itself such a stroke of luck that nothing must be let go. She loved wild buttercups and blood-red anemones. She was friends with the flowers too.

I met her eight years ago in somewhat worldly circumstances, surrounded by famous artists and important gallerists. Everyone was talking but her. She had planted herself with her back to the crowd, facing an enormous fireplace. And she watched the fire without moving. She watched it with such intensity I didn't dare approach her. I had read some of her writing: remarkable poems, and an interview with Hans Ulrich Obrist that had impressed me with the level of her point of view on the world. Here was an artist, to be sure, but as young people say these days, "not just." It's this "not just" that I wanted to know.

It was while working on an issue of *L'Entretien* with my companion, Alain, that we started down a path of friendship. At first, we came to ask questions. Very soon we were coming back to see her, to be with her, to be in the delight of being with her.

The years passed, always with visits at Etel's to talk about the salt of life and the beauty of the world.

When Bernard Comment asked me who I had in mind for a book with an artist, I immediately thought of Etel. And I knew it would be joyful, truthful, intense. I had just finished a book with Christian Boltanski, a conceptual artist if ever there was, who proved to be an adorable man and a bon vivant. We (I) too often think artists are pure spirits, that the flesh has little place in their approach.

With Etel, I knew she would speak about her emotions as the basis of her creation. I have been surprised beyond what I thought possible. Re-creation. Recreation. It was a series of illuminating moments, thanks to the help of her companion, Simone, where I entered the universe of her imagination. You will discover what ensued in these exchanges: humble, impulsive, sincere.

Laure Adler
February 2022

1.

LAURE ADLER: Etel, you are a writer, a poet, an artist; you were born in Lebanon. In which language were you brought up?

ETEL ADNAN: I'm a bit of a particular case, especially for the time. My mother was Greek, from Smyrna (now Izmir), which is to say from Turkey, and my father was born in Damascus; he was also an officer of the Ottoman Empire, so the common language between them was Turkish. We spoke Turkish in Beirut, at home, but my mother spoke to me in Greek, naturally. I grew up this way until the age of twenty, until twenty-four even, speaking Greek and Turkish, and French, because at the time the schools were strictly French speaking; Arabic wasn't taught. I "caught"—as the saying goes—my Arabic in the street and with other children. So, I grew up in four languages.

LA: At what point did you realize you were an artist?

EA: Much later. I was already thirty years old. I was in America. I was there pursuing a doctorate at Berkeley, and two or three years later I got a job—a position teaching philosophy at a college. And since I taught philosophy of art, the person in charge of the art department—because in America, fortunately, art is taught at the same level as philosophy or biology—said to me: "How can you teach philosophy of art without practicing an art?" She encouraged me: "Come, come to the department, you'll find all the materials for art-making." I went there during my free time and at the end of several months, looking at my work, she declared: "You know, your mind is innately developed, you don't need classes." And I became a painter . . . like that.

LA: So, a late revelation?

EA: Yes, and it must have also solved a language problem, because I had gone to the Sorbonne before. I had to go from French to English, and it took me several years to really think comfortably in English.

LA: You're of a generation where there were not many women at university, since you were born in 1925. How did you manage to break into these circles? There must not have been many of you girls . . .

EA: You're perfectly right, at Berkeley in particular. At the Sorbonne there were lots of young girls and women. When I got to Paris in September of 1949, it was really the post-war era. People were still plagued by the war, they talked about it incessantly. Maybe not directly, but they'd say to you: "In times of war, you must do this, or do that." My landlady, especially, spoke of it often.

So, there were lots of girls at the Sorbonne, but at Berkeley it was the opposite. There were only a few young girls and very few women professors. For example, Laura Nader, sister of the Lebanese American polemicist and politician Ralph Nader, was a longtime professor of anthropology at Berkeley, and she often talked about how she was one of the first female professors there. During the mid-1960s there was a young woman at my college who wanted to pursue a PhD in history, and the department head told her "You know, I wouldn't advise it. We don't want women in my department." I also taught for a year in New Haven; there were only two women in my department. A young woman named Annie Scholhar, who incidentally wrote a novel about those years, and me. And we were really ignored. When we asked questions, the teachers and students didn't even respond. It was the revolution of the mid-1960s that really changed these mentalities, somewhat for Black people and a great deal for women.

LA: You were a pioneer, a pioneer both creatively and in what you taught in art history.

EA: Absolutely, at the college there were several women instructors, but not at the level of a large university.

LA: In certain of your books, you explain that you have never studied art but that you often went to museums, and I believe the Louvre, more particularly, and the Venus de Milo were crucial in your awakening to art?

EA: Exactly. When I was a student in Paris, I lived on campus at first, and then in the rue de Tournon, and I often cut classes. I was in the streets. For me Paris was the city, it was life. Studying didn't interest me as much as it did other students, who devoted their days to it. I spent my days in the streets going all over town, on foot, and often I wound up at the Louvre. I had never seen paintings before. There were no museums in Beirut. Today there are exhibitions, but at the time there was nothing. I grew up in a house where there was no telephone, no radio, we went everywhere on foot.... I don't regret any of this, it's just to explain the revelation that painting was for me in France, even more since I was taking classes on aesthetics with professor Souriau. To go to the Louvre for me was like going to the movies. I didn't think of painting in any special way, I simply looked. I remember my very first visit. In the entryway there was the Winged Victory of Samothrace at the stop of the stairs, and it was a revelation. And then the Venus de Milo, the first few times I circled round it like a moth round a light. It's an extraordinary work, a revelation as well. How could this object be of flesh and of stone at the same time? That's the genius of Greek sculpture.

LA: And then very quickly too, during this same period, the discovery of Miró?

EA: Miró was everywhere in Paris at the beginning of the 1960s. In a gallery on the rue Bonaparte, four out of five paintings, especially prints and lithographs, were by Miró. Miró and Picasso were the two great painters that dominated Paris when I was a student.

LA: Where did the desire to paint come from, for you?

EA: I know that when, in that famous art department at the American university, the professor told me to come paint, she put me in a room full of windows with a table that took up an entire wall, and on the other side there was a little stream, surrounded by nature. American campuses have the marvelous feature of being built among trees, most often. In that room there were canvases, paper, brushes, knives. When I took a sheet of paper—not a canvas—she gave me tubes of colored paint, little tubes left lying on the ground. Right away I found what's known as a palette knife—a painter's knife, not a kitchen knife—and I think the object itself, by its nature, allows you to make only flat shapes. So, I didn't start painting with a brush. The brush came later for drawings. I really began with this knife, and it has remained my instrument. The tool you use directs what you do considerably. There is a collaboration between the objects that you use, and this is true beyond painting. It's true even in cooking, it's true with clothes: if you have silk fabric, you're going to make a different dress than if your fabric is linen. It's the same with art: if you use a painter's knife, you're not going to make very precise little lines. And it's the same thing in music: if you play the violin, it's not like playing the piano. I'm very sensitive to the role of objects in our lives, to the importance of this collaboration. That's how it is: the fact that I always use a knife explains why I've made flat color blocks. At first, I made them very naturally, as they came, instinctually. It's like with children—you don't teach them drawing; they paint naturally. We paint naturally, like we speak. This was incidentally the philosophy of that professor. She said: "Everyone can paint, just as everyone can speak." This doesn't mean that everyone is Picasso, but it's a language.

LA: Your paintings don't have titles. Why?

EA: I think titles are either too simple—if it's a mountain, we say "Title: Mountain"—or they're impossible. How to title an abstract painting? An abstract painting is like music, which doesn't really call for a title—we say "sonata"—and abstraction is visual music. It's the same, it has a meaning not destined to be put into words. When I was a professor of philosophy of art, I had students who told me: "This picture has no meaning," and it was very hard to explain the abstract to them without nattering on or making things up. So, I would respond: "Look, when you listen to Beethoven, for example, you don't say that it has no meaning, but you don't explain it either." The same goes for an abstract painting. It's not made to be translated into words.

LA: I have in front of me a print of painting 38, from the catalog of an exhibition at Galerie Lelong—so no title, only "oil on canvas, 34.5 x 45 cm." This is how you name your paintings. I myself can see many things here, but you—what do you see in this painting, which is one of your recent works?

EA: I see memories of landscapes, but not memories of specific landscapes, more like memories of a region. I lived for half a century just north of San Francisco, four kilometers from the ocean, and I saw the bay from my windows, so it involves an accumulation of experiences . . .

LA: A bit like Cézanne.

EA: Yes, yes! I mean, Cézanne could not escape the mountain. It's not even a choice, the mountain is so extraordinary that it asserts itself. And I had a mountain in my window, but this mountain was surrounded by the bay on one side, by the ocean on the other. So, it's not only the mountain, but also the whole "country," the space, if you will; all this region that I saw constantly for years. And I suppose these are impressions that somehow record themselves in the cells of our brain, that come back to me whether I want them or not.

LA: It's the remembrance of the experience of this Californian landscape that returns in your studio?

EA: It's the remembrance of a life of impressions. It's a cumulative experience, it's not a precise place. Even when I mention the mountain, this mountain had infinite points of view: you went around it, you climbed it. It comes back to me most often the way I saw it from my windows. I can draw it with my eyes closed, I saw it so many times. But I was closer to the mountain than Cézanne was. Cézanne went to see it, whereas I had it in my bay window. I couldn't see anything else. My paintings are compositions that reflect, that visually translate diverse experiences. I can't tell you it's this or that place. It's a collage of these places.

LA: What's very impressive in your approach as a painter—we'll return to the importance of poetry and writing in your trajectory—is how emotion, the impression of a landscape and its translation, structure themselves in your thought. Your works are fairly small; you don't make large paintings into which one might have the sense of being able to enter, physically. No, we enter, but by a kind of concentration . . .

EA: The formats are small, but the feeling isn't small. That's very important, and I don't do it on purpose. I understood this intellectually when, at the start of my time in California, I saw some Japanese stamps, little postage stamps, and in these tiny little stamps there were such immense landscapes! This surprise has stayed with me. Now, this doesn't mean I do it consciously—I don't work as consciously as that. There is a truth in oneself. One must make do with that, and it comes out. Fortunately for me, my paintings had to be small because I always worked at home on a relatively small table. And I always had back pain as well. I have trouble moving in that way and I made very few big canvases, but the feeling I want to get across isn't small. It's landscapes and it's the mystery of art. You control without controlling, and the vast landscape is there in these little paintings.

LA: Do you work every day?

EA: No, I've never done anything systematically. I think never in my life have I said that I was busy. When something is asked of me, I'm available. It's a quality of character, not an effort. It makes it so that if I'm invited to dinner, I can go. When I can travel, I don't say: "No, now I've got to work"; I travel. I had many odd jobs before becoming a professor. I took things as they came. Sometimes—I don't know why, maybe I have something to write, or an event I need to participate in, or perhaps someone tells me: "You know, we need a piece for a magazine," and I write a three-page text. The editor tells me: "No, it's too short, you have to write more," so I set myself to writing every day and I write a book called *Paris, When it's Naked*. Chance plays an immense role in our lives. We think we're directing things, but we're also directed by what's happening around us.

LA: Gaston Bachelard spoke of the porousness between dream and painting, literature, and art. Are you one of his followers?

EA: When I was a student at the Sorbonne, from 1949 to 1953, my two favorite professors were Souriau, the director of the thesis I never finished, and Bachelard. I took his courses, one of which made a big impression on me, on the notion of experience. Bachelard was very famous at the time. I think he's a great philosopher that we don't read enough. I'd compare him in importance to Heidegger because what I like in Heidegger is that, despite this feeling of constant abstraction, there is a sensitivity to the world, and Bachelard has this supreme quality—a sensitivity to the world—in plain evidence. Bachelard opened up ideas of poetry through his studies of childhood. He is a great poet-philosopher of poetry, very modern in this respect. There are two French thinkers, in my view, who directly or indirectly said amazing things: Bachelard and Malraux. Malraux is a great thinker of art, everyone knows this, and Bachelard just as much.

LA: Do you agree on the importance of the dream as a creative realm? Do you look to your dreams and to what might happen without you knowing?

EA: Without my knowing, maybe; surely; but I think everything is creation. Life is creation. We call it thinking because it's more precise. It's communication when one thinks. But it's as if to say: night and day. Yes, we are living, everything is life and life takes certain forms, like electricity, like love; it makes you hot, it makes you cold, you love a tree; it comes from the same thing. And thought, poetry, even the act of walking—for me everything holds together. There is no break. We're in a continuum. That's it, the universe: a continuum in every direction, even the empty spaces are not empty; and this is what Bachelard says, he had this feeling of the cosmic where everything holds together.

Logical differences have been created for instruction. That is to say, in order to teach, one makes categories, as Aristotle made categories. But the unfortunate thing is that we've taken these categories to be absolute, separated, when in fact they are not separated, and Bachelard is in this continuum as if inside of a sphere. You go in all directions simultaneously and you choose. For instance, I see this glass of water, but the whole room is present, this glass isn't in a void. I speak of the glass, but it doesn't exist alone. Nothing exists alone; everything is connected. It's inside connections, it seems to me, that we function.

LA: And inside these fields of sensation, how do you choose your mode of expression? Why, from time to time, is it poetry? Why, at other moments, is it literature or philosophy? And why could it be painting?

EA: I began as an undergraduate in literature and philosophy, and Gabriel Bounoure (he's known among certain poets in France; he wrote introductions for Max Jacob and Henri Michaux, among others) was my professor, because he had founded a department, a literary institute, in Beirut, for the "license" [like a bachelor's degree.–Ed.]. It didn't exist before that; there was the Jesuit university in Beirut where all subjects were taught except literature and philosophy. And Gabriel Bounoure, who was sent there by the ministry of foreign affairs, had come as superintendent of French language education in Syria and Lebanon. In 1944, when Lebanon became independent, his position came to an end, and he thought: I must start an institute. Because he was in love with poetry, that's what interested him most, and he didn't want a Catholic institution to teach literature and philosophy, he wanted it to stay totally independent. And then of course after, when he left, they added these two missing subjects to the curriculum at the Université Saint-Joseph.

Gabriel Bonoure taught poetry classes all the time, for the love of it, for pleasure, without looking at the time. For instance, during the Easter vacation, he arrived at two in the afternoon; at five the class was still going, and no one left. He talked, starting with Gérard de Nerval; he read *Les Chimères*, gave commentary, asked questions of the students, and continued with Baudelaire, always Baudelaire. We were being enlightened; we had known nothing and suddenly we read these texts that opened a world to us. So, we were practically electrified by philosophy and poetry. There were twelve pupils to begin with, and the school grew bit by bit. You realize, to have the luck to meet someone like this, who spoke of poetry for hours and who listened, who asked us questions, who knew each of us personally.

Under his influence I began to write poetry, and I wrote a poem at around twenty years old, entitled "The Book of the Sea," because at the time Beirut was a small town—you saw the sea from everywhere. I never published this poem, and then later, when I left for America, I was facing a new language. It never even occurred to me that I didn't know English. It took me a semester and then I myself was teaching in English. And that was when I became a painter.

During the Vietnam War, the importance of poetry in the antiwar movement in America was tremendous. American poets today never talk about it; they've put aside this period which was a great awakening of poetry. There's a spirit of rebellion in the pioneers of that new poetry like Allen Ginsberg. He was a complete poet, at once lyrical and political. He takes it further; for him, poetry speaks to the entire American culture and the lived reality of Americans. One day, spontaneously, I began to militate against the war. I was horrified by the images of the Vietnam War. I think at the time there was less censorship of images of war. Later, when governments saw the importance of images to public opinion, they became cautious. But at the time the war was broadcast live, and I saw with my own eyes American soldiers with flamethrowers burning Vietnamese villages. You couldn't . . . you couldn't not look. The entire country reacted to these images because they went beyond political analyses. When you see a real war broadcast live, every day, it becomes unbearable. You don't think any more about the reasons for or against. That's when I wrote my first poems, and since they were accepted very quickly, I felt like I fit in with American poetry.

LA: You've published poetry in different languages and especially in English, which is how the world first came to know your poetic work, in America first. I'm going to read a small excerpt of a book entitled *There*, translated from the American. Here is what you write, Etel:

> Listen, listen if you care (or if you don't), do not mistake wine for food, do experience fear outside your mother's womb, remember with your guts, speak from my own heart, extricate yourself, if you can, from my rage.

> There, along the white marble climbing toward heaven and through a sky darkened with airplanes, listen, there's noise, the gates to nothingness are open while you struggle, and stutter, and I speak with no voice.

EA: Yes.... What can I tell you?

LA: No, I only wanted us to listen to what you write.

Your poems are often fragmentary. They are manifestly products of association. They can speak of geographical continents very far from one another, and they also speak a lot about war, not only the Vietnam war but also in Lebanon.

EA: Yes, necessarily, because I've always thought one is traversed by what one lives through. I'm asked sometimes: "Why is there so much history of contemporary war in your poetry?" I've answered: "Because it's not me that writes it, it's history that writes it." I have often wanted to think of something besides war, but always another conflict arose. I was born into a family where there were only three of us. My father was an officer of the empire, classmate of Mustafa Kemal Ataturk, the founder and first president of the Republic of Turkey. My father had been at the battle of the Dardanelles. At thirty-eight years old his career was over; the Ottoman Empire had disappeared. So, he was a man whose life was somewhat tragic, by reason of history. My mother was much less cultivated than my father, but even more viscerally attached to her Greek world in Turkey. She saw Smyrna burn when she was only twenty-four years old. She thought only of Smyrna. She had stayed there, mentally. When I would go walking along the corniche in Beirut, along the waterfront, I would see huge clouds on the horizon and I would say to my mother, to make her happy: "Is that Smyrna?" I heard talk only of Smyrna. Her friends came to the house and always repeated: "The grapes were better in Smyrna; the fish was better in Smyrna . . . " She was possessed. She was exiled from her daily life, and she lived in the absence of this city. Her family dispersed: one brother in Salonika, one brother in Cyprus, one brother in Alexandria, a sister in Italy. You see, wars are explosions of families, of lives; and I lived in this repetition of history at home, these stories of interminable war.

We spoke Greek and Turkish in our home. My father didn't speak Greek. But my mother spoke Greek to me very naturally, because it was really the language she knew best. She also spoke a bit of French, and she had learned Turkish, since she was born there. And there were two religions at home: my father was Muslim; my mother was Greek Orthodox. I think I've been very lucky to have grown up considering the world to be inhabited by different kinds of people. It's an advantage, on account of it being natural.

It wasn't something you had to figure out. You even expected that suddenly someone might show up who wasn't quite the same as what you already knew. The Near East in those days was a stopping-off point. It was the end of an empire, with a changing population, and school was French. Under the mandate, we were forbidden to speak Arabic, even at home. I learned it later, haphazardly, in the street. I regret that, by the way. I would have liked to know it better. Anyway, I went to the convent school. The education was very strict. These were very good schools, but they were also a bit narrow. They would say: "Poor little Etel, everything is as it should be, but her father is Muslim." We were told that Muslims couldn't get into Heaven .... I learned to think critically, because at home I heard another side of the story. It was the Greek world; things were more accepted. I was an only child. We would go to Damascus to visit my aunt. There it was still the Ottoman Empire. It was another world, the end of a world. And even in Beirut, there was the cosmopolitan neighborhood where I lived, which was no longer solely Christian.

We never went to the other side of the boulevard because we had nothing to do there. There were two or three tramway lines, but we got around on foot most of the time. There were three taxis; you hailed them by pointing a finger. I consider all of that to be a poetic world. Because it was innocent. Everything was in a minor mode. There was no pollution. We were coming out of the Great War; it had taken years. We didn't know where the world was headed; we didn't think it was headed anywhere. We lived each day by itself. We knew only the present. It was an idyllic world, and I was of the first generation of girls to be allowed to swim. I lived through the liberation of women: a very interesting question, because it's the result of little jumps, as if you were jumping a few meters at a time. At first, there were ten or so little girls who went swimming. Not more than that. And then suddenly, you saw women eating ice cream in the ice cream shop. That's how it took place. In little stages.

LA: What's amazing with you, Etel, is your feeling that the beauty of the world is real. Moreover, you've celebrated it your whole life, whether it be in poetry, painting, or calligraphy. And I think when you were little, your parents put you in the garden and you spoke to the flowers.

EA: Yes. At one time, my parents rented a large house, and I remember my mother telling me: "You sit on the stool and don't move." So, I was sitting there like that, for an hour or two, and since I had no brother or sister, I would speak aloud, I would communicate with the garden. There was also a cat, who belonged to my mother, not to me. The house was her house. For Greek wives, the house belongs to them. It doesn't belong to the family; it belongs to the wife. Fathers bleed themselves dry to buy a house for their daughter. If they can't buy a house, they buy an armoire. You see? The daughter must be given a foundation. It's more than an object. Therefore, we were in my mother's house. That really affected me, and it made it so that I spent my life outside, in cafés and traveling. I was never really at home indoors. This is how I was raised: "Don't move, don't touch. We're cleaning the house."

LA: What did you say to the flowers, then?

EA: I believe the nuns spoke to us about miracles. The education we had was a kind of irrationalism—sometimes charming, sometimes terrifying. We spoke of things that were completely invisible. Paradise, saints, sins; it easily prepares you for a world that's a bit surrealist. And I think I was there, dreaming that I worked miracles. What miracles? For example, I would give agency to flowers. Suddenly they could reply to me. These days, being an only child is almost the rule. But in my generation, at school, I was the only girl with neither brother nor sister. So, I watched the world. The world kept me company. I observed. I wanted to step on my own shadow. When returning home from the beach, the sun was such that my shadow was in front of me, and I wanted to step on it. This could be a poem in itself. We don't need to add a thing. To observe the world is poetry. The world is exciting and when you don't have lots of other children around, you speak to yourself, you look around more.

Then the Second World War began. My parents were broke, and at sixteen, I went to work in an office while studying for my two baccalaureate exams, at school or in private tutorial. And there, work was a huge discovery. Especially at a time when women were still at home. The world of work is really a second birth. In the first place, you meet people who aren't friends of your parents. You're a girl, and you speak to boys. You earn money, even if my mom took it from me, because girls gave their money to the family. You realize, all of this during my own lifetime. It's an extraordinary reservoir of poetry. For Beirut, the war was a boom, since wars make fortunes for many people. Everything changes; everything moves very fast. I followed the war with my cohort at the office. We had tacked up a map of the battle of Stalingrad on a large wall.

I was even at a press conference that de Gaulle gave in Beirut, and I recorded the conference in shorthand with the secretary of the chief of staff. I was busy, but in a positive way; it was much more interesting than school or home. I had the sense of being active in history, of living it. And then there was the war with Nasser in 1956; the coup d'état in Beirut in 1958; the war of 1967; the civil war from 1975 to 1990. For fifteen years we spent our time listening to the war on the radio, so how could I not think about it?

I'm like an antenna that picked up what was happening in the world, and suddenly I didn't want to write anymore. I had nothing to say. Our life is determined by big decisions, but on the inside life isn't determined. You can do something this afternoon that you didn't plan to do. You can meet someone who will suddenly change your life without your having known it a few minutes prior. So, chance—whether it be inside a painting or in daily life or in artistic decisions—chance collaborates with us.

2.

LA: With what element do you begin a painting?

EA: At first, since I had these little ends of pastels, I'd start with a red square. And this red square called for the gestures that followed. That's how it is. That is, you make a mark, and the mark creates a situation, and this situation calls for other gestures. And it comes along, and you learn as you go.

LA: But you always start off with a color?

EA: Yes, indeed, I start with colors, it's true.

LA: What is color?

EA: I've had a somewhat philosophical year, and I got excited again re-reading a book by Deleuze on Nietzsche. I also re-discovered an interest in Nietzsche, which I had never lost . . . you know, Nietzsche gave us interpretive schemas and concepts, and one of these concepts is the *will to power*. Well, I discovered that color was the manifestation, the expression, of the will to power of matter. This is what great philosophers do: they furnish you with essential tools for thought that are very powerful. So there: color. Color is an affirmation of presence so strong that it's almost alive, almost human. There's a power in color. My friend Yvon Lambert came over the other day with a bouquet of peonies, and peonies are deeper than roses. They have a certain color—I'd almost say blacker, more assertive. It's interesting. What's beautiful, too, is the mixing of color. Since I had no formal training in art, no one taught me how to marry colors. Painter friends told me: "But you never mix these colors, you don't juxtapose them. How do you dare do that?" Because no one told me not to do it. I don't see why I couldn't. They have preconceived ideas. Mixing colors is very engaging because you witness the birth of a new color. It's really a birth, like a child arriving. You put in a particular red, you put in a white, and you have a pink that you've never seen before and that helps with the following stage. In fact, I play by ear, as they say.

LA: You mean that colors speak to you, then?

EA: That's right, they speak to me, there they are. I deal with them. I answer them. There's a discourse between the self and the white paper on which you work. There is a discourse. It's thrilling. You strike out into an unknown that renews itself nonstop. You never know what you can do unless you try. You have to try.

I had a purely literary education, very literary. But that helps in doing another art. Whether it be music or poetry, it helps. It trains you. They're the same problems. They're problems of composition and of confidence. When you walk down the street, you don't think about the next step; you go for it. It's the same with work. You begin and you continue. You must have confidence. You can't have criticism intervening during the work. You have to leave criticism for later on. And then you need a certain modesty. This is what I can do. I'm obliged to accept it. It's me.

LA: And you've never lost that, your self-confidence?

EA: No.

LA: Against your mother, then?

EA: No, no, I haven't lost it because I forge ahead.

LA: What does that mean?

EA: It's my character. A friend from junior high school told me: "You walk like a bull, headfirst," and it's true. You've got to . . . I've awakened a desire to paint, which was there before. You mustn't kill that; you've got to accept it.

LA: Does it need to be maintained as well?

EA: You need to maintain it by working. Above all, you can't listen to people. It depends on whom, but don't listen to people who are too negative.

LA: But for a long time, you exhibited very little?

EA: Yes, for a very long time I barely exhibited.

LA: You weren't missing that?

EA: No, it didn't stop me. In life, two or three people whose opinions matter are sufficient, and that often helps you to continue.

LA: Were you yourself surprised by what you made, Etel?

EA: I was a little bit in a fairy-tale. Yes, I was in a world of beauty. I had no problems at the college. I wasn't censored. I wasn't criticized. Simone, with whom I lived, began to take sculpture classes. I encouraged her because one day, in the kitchen, I saw her holding some eggplants, but with such a fusion between her and these two objects that I thought to myself: she's a sculptor, she has the touch.
   Me, it was painting and color. Painting is an intellectual mystery and when you love poetry or ideas, philosophy, painting isn't far. It's closer than sculpture. You don't know what it is. The fact of not knowing isn't discouraging. You like not knowing. It's nice not to know. You don't know what it is. Let's keep a bit of mystery to things. You don't know. You get pleasure from not knowing. In the word "to know" [*savoir*], there's the word "to have" [*avoir*], and you have nothing. You have very little. You have nothing. In fact, all human beings are mystics because they know nothing. They don't know; they forge ahead.

LA: And it's from this nothing that you can begin to create?

EA: Yes. You need courage all the same. This is why I say: you trust. The word "trust" is important. You trust; you are in confidence.

LA: In yourself, with yourself?

EA: With yourself, with the world, with the people you like; let's go. You trust in yourself. Yes, this is the most important because you can't distance yourself easily from yourself. You may as well make do. There's nothing else.

LA: But we women. Our mothers didn't really raise us to have trust in ourselves.

EA: It's true. Look at gallerists for example. Mine were often women, and I noticed in their way of thinking of their trade that they did it mostly because it gave them access to interesting men. Architects, interesting clients; they preferred to deal with them than with another woman. I really noticed that they weren't that proud to have a woman artist. They preferred the gentlemen. This came from the gallerist, not from the public, and it's true that, until very recently, it has been harder for women to make it. And I'd say especially in the arts. Because there's this intellectual side that seemed to be reserved for men, and also because of the history of art. All our models are male: Picasso, Miró, Paul Klee, Kandinsky, and many others. So, you can't escape it. Never women . . . . When you were given a compliment, it was condescending, as in: "I want to tell you that what you're doing is good." As if giving you a gift. And you get used to that. It's every day. But that doesn't prevent you from working.

LA: At what age did you begin to draw the bottles? Very young?

EA: At maybe seven or eight years old. It's the light on the bottles that interested me. The glints of sun on the bottles.

I liked to draw. And I liked the compass. To draw circles. Yes, I drew a lot. For example, we were told: "Draw the lid of your pencil box." We had pencil boxes. I loved pencil boxes. And I drew circles. I also liked writing very early on.

LA: Did you like to read early on as well?

EA: Very little. Very little, because there were no books in the house. Nor in the houses I visited. Neither in French nor in Arabic. There were no books.

LA: Your mother didn't read?

EA: Yes, she had three or four Greek novels that she reread. There were always the gospels. My father knew the Qur'an by heart. He never stopped reading it. And that's about it. The first book I read was *Michel Strogoff*—not bad. It really struck me. It's funny. I remember in the Catholic school where I was a student, there was a bookcase, and I said to the nun: "I want that book." She replied: "No you're too little. It's not for you." It was the Revelation of Saint John. She didn't give it to me. She said no. She told me: "There's another book next to it, let's see what that is." It was *Michel Strogoff* ... but no, really, I didn't read much. And then poetry awakened me to the world because Gabriel Bounoure emphasized poetry. I know Gérard de Nerval by heart. I know Baudelaire practically by heart. But I liked Apollinaire very much, right away. It's beautiful. "La Chanson du mal-aimé" is mesmerizing. Great poetry is mesmerizing. See what happens when you recite "Le Bateau ivre." We rehearsed and rehearsed it. It was extraordinary. Bounoure liked Michaux very much. That took me more time. He wasn't my favorite poet. No, I liked Apollinaire much better.

LA: When did you understand that you yourself could also write poetry?

EA: Oh, I never thought that! I have never said I was a poet for instance; except when I wrote my first poem, I was twenty years old. It was the marriage of the sun and the sea. And it's funny, my most recent poems have nearly the same themes as the first ones, which never became books; they have not been published.

LA: Why is it, do you think, that we have a "need for poetry," to use Yves Bonnefoy's expression?

EA: You have a need to free things up, to put in order, to clear away nonessential things to make room in your head so that an image can take its place. For me, that's what poetry is. It's when your attention recovers and rests. We live between veils, it seems to me. Nowadays I need to go out to dinner to find myself—I'm so outside of myself. We live outside ourselves. We rarely have moments where music or poetry provide relief. Even if it requires a lot of attention, it's a relief, because it empties the mind. In the true sense of the word. Music and poetry manifest in the mind. We need poetry amid this chaos and chatter.

LA: You speak of "putting in order."

EA: In the best sense, that is, to empty out. Throwing out. I love throwing out. My girlfriend, Simone, hates it. I love it. We argue. I even take advantage when she's not around to get rid of things. Because you need mental space. Cleaning the house means throwing things out. We are eaten up by objects and we become babysitters of our houses. So, you've got to clear away: that's what it is to put in order.

LA: What else do you have when you're an artist?

EA: I think when you're an artist, you have something more, an opening. Even a bad painter has something more than a critic, for instance, because he knows from inside the problems involved in his approach. It's an asset. There's a pleasure to art which must be particular, because people who aren't artists or poets feel it and begrudge us; they know we have a certain world that they do not. They like for artists to be poor, since deep down they know they're missing something. There is a deep pleasure in mixing colors. It's also an intellectual pleasure, a total pleasure, a far-reaching one.

LA: Which gives you the most pleasure: writing or painting?

EA: They're two different worlds. Even if they meet because they spring from the same person. When I devote myself to one, I don't think about the other, so I can't say. There have been times when I didn't write because I had a problem with the language. I arrived in 1955 in America, and I published my first poem in English in 1965. And during those ten years, I didn't write. I was coming from

French, and I was learning English. That's when I became a painter. It wasn't planned. Unconsciously, painting replaced writing.

LA: Could one say that writing brushes the abyss and is often on the darker side, the dramatic, while painting is on the side of fullness?

EA: It's physical, yes. There's a kind of sport to it—you feel it more, the body participates, you move your hand, you stand up. You're physically immobile when you paint, which is also the case with writing, but once you've begun, you get carried away. And then in my history, there have been many tragedies. First the war: I started to write against the Vietnam war spontaneously. My first poem dates to 1965. Writing is social right away; words are more attached to history than colors are. There's the history of painting, of course, but that's something else; you don't begin with that, you begin with lines, with shapes . . . . So, in my case, writing has been more tragic, more linked with the real world, while painting is exhilarating.

LA: The engine of writing is anger?

EA: It's anger. It's engagement—not engagement in political parties, but it's still an engagement in the world as it is. It's hard to step out of that. Whereas there's an innocence in the fact of painting that's restful to me.

LA: Hope?

EA: Hope, I don't know, because it's very tied to the moment when you make the painting. You don't have a sense of the future when you're painting. It's like when you do laundry or when you eat. It's very immediate. Thinking projects itself better into the future and the past.

LA: Do you think beauty still has a future? Because nature isn't looking so well these days . . .

EA: We have to be careful. It's the future that concerns us most of all. There's still a lot of beauty in the world, but there's no place, even the most beautiful place, that doesn't remind us of the danger there. We don't have that total innocence anymore. In the forests, we see the paths crossed by train tracks. We see the suburbs spreading out. Even in Paris there is such crowding. So, we're seldom completely in nature. We're already at the beginning of the danger. It's very real.

LA: The beauty of the world. You might say that this is it, one of your principal themes, the beauty of the world?

EA: The beauty of the world. The world is beautiful. The colors of the Mediterranean: it's a miracle, it's so beautiful. The dark blue of the Mediterranean, it's unbelievable.

LA: Have you gazed as much at the Mediterranean Sea as at your mountain?

EA: Yes, all told, yes. My first passion was the Mediterranean. The mountain came home to me. It was in front. And the mountain was a reference point for me. I needed that, psychologically. It's very beautiful, that little mountain. But between San Francisco and Canada there's a series of incredible mountains—you see them from the plane. You pass next to them and you're below the summit.

LA: You mean to say that these are almost primitive landscapes that live in our imagination?

EA: They're primitive. Like images buried in our memory. And suddenly, they're in front of us. This moves us because of an overwhelming impact. Unforgettable, like love at first sight. It's the same. It's love at first sight. And it's unimaginable. I would like to have seen the Landes. I also read, not long ago, a text on Argentina, where they have buildings in the vineyards—a special architecture for the barrels and the wine. And it overwhelmed me, almost as if I had visited in person.

LA: Where would you still like to go?

EA: I'd like to go to Guatemala. I was supposed to go and couldn't because I would have had to miss a week of classes. I didn't dare and I really regretted it. There are beautiful volcanoes in Guatemala that I've seen in pictures. And it's a country where there are weavers, as in the time of the Spanish conquest. There are many women who make weaving. I've noticed that the motifs are the same as in Morocco. Spanish Arabs must have been brought over by the conquistadors, on the ships, because they were never sure of their conversion. We don't know. The jewelry is very Moroccan, too. I would have liked to go to Argentina. I would have liked to go back to Northern Italy. I love Verona and Padua. A lot, a lot. And I loved San Gimignano, the towers. The towers are magical. They say they were for defending the town. I doubt that very much. There's a mystical geometry behind these things. Venice you can never forget.

LA: We say, "contemplate a landscape." Do you think this is the right expression?

EA: The word "contemplate" is still a difficult word. Yes, I've contemplated. I've gazed at my mountain, but more than anything, I've walked all over it. I went often. It made its way into my house, into me. It was facing me. I couldn't look at anything else. You couldn't escape it. I didn't seek it out, but I mean . . . there it was. The mountain isn't simply a mountain. It was my reference point. At first, when I looked at it, I felt soothed.

LA: It's your companion, then?

EA: Right, I felt myself not in exile, not a foreigner. It's really someone that I had met.

LA: Someone?

EA: Yes, yes. When we talk about love, why do we always think of people? Why not love something else? I think you can love your piano if you're a pianist.

LA: You don't miss the mountain?

EA: A lot, I miss it a lot. I miss America. I miss California. The light. The people. It's the whole thing.

LA: You felt good there?

EA: I felt good there.

LA: And here, less good?

EA: It's less exciting. I really have a hard time ... things are formal here. France isn't easy. It's basically a country of schoolteachers. "Don't do this; do that." There's less freedom and more hierarchy, and perhaps less desire as well. Maybe this is the influence of Catholicism? It's a country that was once considered Jansenist, where the concept of sin and authority dominated. Someone once said to me, "you're really going to like this gentleman, he's a 'monsieur de,' an aristocrat." But today it doesn't mean anything to be an aristocrat. He's a "monsieur de." So, you see what I mean? There's a feeling, an acceptance, of authority and hierarchy.

LA: Do you feel yourself to be in exile here, in France, Etel?

EA: I feel like I'm in exile, maybe not in a traditional way, but because I miss many things. When you talk about things you miss, it's also the things you didn't do that you are missing.

LA: But isn't it by missing that we create?

EA: Yes, in a certain way; that is, when you don't know what to do, you start writing or painting. It fills a need in that sense.
   Painting has become a need. You feel that you want to paint. It's in the fingers. I don't know where it is, but it's there.

LA: Haven't you painted this morning?

EA: Today, no, but usually, I wake up and it's at that moment … ah, but yes, I did finish a painting I had begun yesterday. Yes, it turns into a need. You don't know why or how. Many things are needful like that. I mean, even eating breakfast when you're not necessarily hungry. You have needs that are more or less strange. For me, it's painting.

LA: Is there a kind of affirmation of the world in your art?

EA: Yes. You don't know what the world really is, but there's a feeling. It's a feeling that pushes to be expressed. It lives in us, this feeling. It's very strong. It's very strong because it's very physical.

LA: Do you believe in the separation of body and soul? Or does everything take place in the body, for you?

EA: I've thought very little about the soul during my existence. I don't know. There are many things like that, which are cultural. But we have an interiority, and we believe this interiority to have a seat, a locus, and this is what we call our soul.

LA: In fact, this interiority might be everywhere, everywhere in the body and not only in what we call the soul.

EA: What we call the soul, we don't know. The separation .... But we land in immortality; do we believe in that? It's strange anyway, for example, the Druze believe in metempsychosis. Do they have the experience of it?

LA: Do you believe in nothingness?

EA: Not really. I understand that sometimes people need to believe they're not going to die. And you know, things have been repeated to us so often that we no longer know what it is to not think about it or believe it. There's a whole affectivity around it. For instance, I have a friend who lost her son. She's Lebanese, and well, she's certain that he's up there, in heaven, waiting for her. And when someone mentions his death, she says, "No, he's not dead." And she believes this so strongly that it's contagious. We don't know. And since we know so little ... I'd rather say I don't think about it, but anything is possible. We don't know.

LA: In one of his books, Vladimir Jankélévitch writes: "It's not worth thinking about death, because we can't think about it."

EA: That's right, we can't think about it. We are there. We've encountered no one who has spoken to us of it, even Lazarus in the gospels. We didn't ask him where he'd been—it's bizarre. Even Jesus—we didn't ask him what he'd been through when he came back to life. *Where were you? What did you do? How was it?* We don't know.

3.

LA: How's life going today, Etel?

EA: It's going slowly. Nothing special. I found some texts by Varèse that I kept for you, for you to read. He was in America at one point in his life. He had been friends with Kiki Smith's mom. Kiki's dad was one of the finest sculptors I've ever seen. And the mom, Jane, was an actress, very close to two friends of ours, Lillian Kieslcr, and her girlfriend Mariette Charton. These two women were truly exceptional, and Kiki's mom would come to New York with them. Frederick Kiesler, the famous architect, died relatively young, but Lillian had been the first assistant to Hans Hofmann, who taught painting to all the American expressionists. It was a very interesting little group, and Tony Smith made bunkcrs in front of and around the Rothko Chapel in Houston—huge granite blocks among the trees . . . . I've never done sculpture myself.

LA: But there aren't painters that have impressed you?

EA: I liked mainstream painters, already well-known, like Nicolas de Staël. I could have met him because he went where I had friends: Suzanne Tézenas, Georges Schehadé and Gabriel Bounoure. I have a Russian friend, Lydia, who tried to sell his paintings. She was unsuccessful and she told Georges Schéhadé: "But Georges, it's cheap, buy this painting from me," and that fool, whose wife had a gallery in Beirut, preferred Georges Mathieu, who's horrible, who's a bad painter. Georges said in front of me and Simone: "Oh, Nicolas de Staël, I'd step right over his paintings. I wouldn't even look at them." He was proud. There's always this vain, stupid side to people.

LA: I'd like us to talk about your poetry today, Etel. When did you start writing?

EA: Like I told you, poetry began because of Gabriel Bounoure. I was twenty years old. He had opened the college of letters, which was a night school. So, I worked during the day and went there afterward. Bounoure loved poetry above all else. Then he left Beirut. He lived in Cairo, and he hated his time there. We continued to write to one another. He thought that poetry was the highest level of the mind. There's a striking poem by Baudelaire where he says his mind is floating on water, on the sea. Bounoure invited André Gide to Beirut in 1947—I remember it as if it were yesterday. It was before I came to Paris. Bounoure awarded scholarships. He was the one who decided, and one day he said to me: "You are one of the new grantees." And so, I told my mother: "I'm going to Paris because Bounoure is giving me a scholarship." She had a doctor friend who was paranoid and who, since he lived alone, kept grenades, real live grenades that explode, to protect himself in case robbers came; and she told me: "I'm going to take one of his grenades and I'm going to kill monsieur Bounoure, because this man is making me crazy. He wants to send you to Paris and in Paris you'll be eaten alive." I went to tell Bounoure's secretary, who relayed the message to him. He had a good laugh. I left for Paris all the same.

LA: But that doesn't say when you began to write poetry?

EA: Well, I wrote a poem about the sea . . . because since I liked the sea so much, I would watch it. And when you watch it, you see the sun's rays penetrate to a certain level, and I wrote a poem that I've never published, called "a bit of marriage of the sun and the sea." It's called "The Book of the Sea." In the Arabic world, a book is called *kitab*, "the book of," as in "The Book of Questions." This poem is still in my desk. And I truly believed I was born to sit on the sidewalks of Beirut, on the ground, and watch. The passersby and the shopkeepers would point at me. They called me "the little madwoman" because I would sit in the street, on a sidewalk, next to the Kurdish women who were looking for work. At the time there were many Kurds who came on foot from Syria, from Turkey, from everywhere. And the women wore colorful clothing. They would sit and wait for a customer to approach them, mostly for washing linens, to do big washes. What really upset me, one day, was I was eating an orange in the street and tossing the peels as I walked, and one of these women rushed after the peel and ate it. They were that poor. This struck me because at the time you couldn't easily take a taxi. Porters carried baskets larger than themselves, and people piled melon after melon onto them. It was so cruel. The customer walked ahead and the Kurd with his huge basket followed, and some were hunchbacked for life from carrying this way. I witnessed this kind of poverty in those days.

LA: After Beirut it was Paris. Did you continue to write poetry?

EA: Yes, in Paris I wrote "The Book of Night." And following that, "The Book of the End." E.N.D. I think even after death, after grief, separations, there's the real end which is forgetting. That's what it is: *La Fin*; the end; these three or four books of poems are at a friend's, who keeps them in a drawer. A friend from the college of letters. He's still alive. He lives in the rue Jacob. He was the director of the Baalbeck Festival, and his father was a poet.

In Beirut, there were poets that France supported by giving them meeting places and grant subsidies. Before I went to Paris, during the war, I worked for the news and radio broadcast service for Free France in Beirut. One of the first directors of that office was Jacques Lassaigne. He had me take dictation of a piece on Honoré Daumier. He really liked Daumier. The reporters played along, but there were some each week that criticized Free France. These were rarely paid, and only when they wrote a favorable article. I could see how even the Allies were shooting themselves in the foot. We had a liaison officer whom I liked, but the bureau chief said to me: "You're talking too much with his secretary." He didn't want me to, because she was Russian . . .

Our mission was to take trucks into the villages; we'd set up a screen to show newsreels of the war, while the war was taking place. At first it was de Gaulle, nonstop, then we showed Churchill some, and a lot of Stalin because de Gaulle really played the Russians against the English. I think he had more affinity for the

Russians than for the English. He detested the Anglo-Saxons. I was supposed to note how things had gone and type up a report. In fact, we made two reports: one true and one false. In the false one, we said that people cheered for de Gaulle and for Churchill too. Now, the young Lebanese didn't like Churchill. But it was the English who paid for the vans and the staff. France had no money. So, I quickly grasped the system. By the third report, I was making them up myself. To make the English attaché believe it was truly the real report, we made carbon copies and numbered them. And I'd give him the eighth copy, for instance. And it was a fake report, where we didn't tell him that people applauded more for Stalin than for Churchill and had covered Beirut with pictures of Stalin at the time. Ah yes, we really favored Russia. All of this was before Yalta. It's when I learned to make things up in writing.

LA: And what were your political opinions at the time?

EA: On the walls at the newspaper, we had enormous maps of Europe, including Russia, and pins with little flags, and we followed the Allied advance, the retreat. We followed the war in North Africa. And it was exciting because we had a cinema service downstairs, with a theater, and they showed films. We followed the war in images. We saw the newsreels. We had a lieutenant called Fleuriot. He'd been parachuted by Free France into France for a special operation, and he died. Everyone wept when we learned the news because he was shortsighted. He had the eyes of a child that wears glasses. It was one of our first deaths.

One day, de Gaulle came with General Catroux, who was the high commissioner of Free France. There was a large meeting at

Catroux's residence, where the New Zealanders and Australians from Palestine were located, since at the time they fought in the English army, especially in North Africa. The international press was there because they had planned to declare or promise independence for Lebanon and Syria. De Gaulle did this because the English had landed. They arrived without a warning; one morning, they entered Syria and Lebanon. And right then, to get them to leave, de Gaulle said: "We must grant independence," and they called the press office where I was stenographer. Mme. Catroux was known in Paris for being very violent; she would yell and scream. So, I went over there, and she scared me! She intimidated me and I cowered in a chair. Then she rang up the office, in front of me, to say: "I asked you for a secretary and here you send me a baby. I'm going to call the chief of staff." I was the baby. A new secretary arrived. Everything I lived through during that time left its mark on me.

It's memorable because wars make and unmake nations. It's because of the Second World War that Beirut became important. The different armies came through the city in their trucks. And then there was a lot of scrap metal; there had been a real war in the Syrian desert, and they had left all the ruined tanks that Lebanese businessmen bought for the iron, which they resold in Romania. Many people enriched themselves.

In Beirut, the windows and shutters had been painted blue. There had been curfews, but no bombardments. The Germans never entered Lebanon. There were some in Syria, with the pro-Vichy forces. Free France, the "real soldiers," came a bit later. It was exciting because that's when they needed secretaries in the offices. And that's how I began work as a stenographer at sixteen, because there was work for girls; women's liberation started with office work. At the time, there were still very few women lawyers and doctors. And that's how Beirut grew rich.

LA: And you, how did you live through this period of women's liberation?

EA: I had a lot of trouble because I wanted to go dancing in the evening and my mother refused. I saw boys all day long at the office, but I couldn't go out dancing with them. I had an Armenian boyfriend who was a jeweler and had friends in the nightclub orchestras, so he'd bring me to the rehearsals, and we'd dance in front of his friends. That way I could get home before nine at night. One day—it was summertime—my mother had gone out and left my father to watch me. I went dancing, but late, and when I arrived home my father was waiting for me outside in the street. So, the young man and I jumped in a taxi and passed by the house many times, and I kept telling him: "He'll wind up going inside eventually." But my boyfriend was scared and kept saying: "It's costing me a fortune; you've got to get out." I got out of the taxi and went inside. My father chased me with his cane around the table as I begged him: "Don't tell mama, don't tell mama!" He said to me: "What does that mean, 'don't tell mama'? What am I??" I wasn't afraid of him. I was afraid he'd tell my mother. This, alas, was the end of the dancing at night.

I was monitored by my family and above all by the neighbors. The neighbors were the real problem. One of them, who was our landlord, came to see my mother one day: "I have something very serious to tell you." She replied, "What is it?" And I heard, "I saw Etel kiss an English soldier under my own window. You must put a stop to this."

My mother had a photographer friend, since at the time women loved to have themselves photographed. All the photographers were Armenians. He was called M. Abel. He lived on the Corniche, in front of the Hotel Saint-Georges, and he had twin daughters. There came a day when he declared to my mother: "I have something very serious to tell you." Sea bathing was in fashion; you rented a changing cabin, you left your clothes inside, and in the water, there were rafts made of wooden boards where you could sit when you got tired. The English soldiers loved to swim. There were lots of them. And M. Abel said to my mother: "I had my twins with me, I was watching the girls. And what do I see? Our little Etel, sitting on the raft, pushing English soldiers into the water with her feet." It was a game. I'd push them off and they'd get back on. I didn't know them, but it was unspoken, we were playing. So, then my mother decreed: "No more swimming this summer." She had to prove to M. Abel that she was an honest woman and that she didn't let her daughter touch English soldiers. I pleaded my cause. I tried to explain to her. I said: "Mama, they were sunburned. You know, they're not like us. Their backs are pink. Their backs get burnt in the sun." That didn't work. That's how it went, "women's liberation." We made a step forward, a step backward. It was really work that gave us our freedom. There was a need for young women, and many young women worked all over. One of these Englishmen, who was in earnest, told me he wanted to marry me and added, "We have a large cotton business in Manchester." He often asked me out for hot chocolate at the Swiss bakery. That was a big outing, and I remember that one day I didn't reply. An Australian officer came by and asked if I wanted to go to the Empire Cinema with him, and I answered: "Yes, tomorrow." I knew three words in English. The next morning, my mother was suspicious; she wasn't happy. I told her: "I'm going to the movies." She asked my father to go with me. In front of the cinema the guy was waiting. He stood behind us and bought the next ticket, and when the film started, he appeared with a little bag of chocolates. So, there was my father, me, and him. He gave me a chocolate, I gave it to my father, and at some point, my father stood up and said: "Where are these chocolates coming from? We didn't come with chocolates," and in the dark he saw this guy with his packet. So, we left. That was the end of the date. This was the kind of thing that happened. My boyfriend, the one who wanted to get married, had been sent to Libya. When he returned, a girl at the office said to me: "You know, I saw Guy yesterday." I thought: Ah, he's in Beirut but he hasn't called me. I phoned him at his office. He tells me: "I came to your house and your mother made me get on my knees and swear not to marry you." Like in the film *The Rose Tattoo*.

LA: You accepted the situation?

EA: But certainly. You accepted everything. You had no autonomy. Our parents took our money. My mother took my money at the end of the month.

LA: You weren't allowed your pocket money, even?

EA: No, we weren't allowed to have our own money. My mother needed it. That was normal, but even so. In 1980 I got to know the singer Fairuz. She once told me, with tears in her eyes, "You know, until now, I have never gotten any of the money the festival paid me. My husband and brother dealt with the contracts in my name and kept the money." She hadn't gotten a penny from the Baalbeck Festival. I recalled my aunt in Damascus telling her woes to my father. This was his sister. She told him: "I can't even buy tobacco to roll a cigarette. He won't let me buy tobacco; he buys it for me." Her husband would go to buy her tobacco, so she didn't have to leave the house. I covered that festival at Beiteddine, and I wrote a piece on Fairouz. It was very moving because all the young men had their lighters held up while she sang, like votive candles in a church. I wrote an editorial on the front page and a journalist sent her my piece. I'd been to see her, and she told me bits about her life. She had a child born with a deformity whom she brought with her on all her travels; she was afraid he might be mistreated in her absence. She had a dreadful husband, an even worse brother-in-law. They wouldn't allow her to sign her contracts.

LA: When did you begin to fear your mother less?

EA: My mother was so severe, and violent in her severity . . . . I left home to go to Paris. I don't know if I had even a little money to get to the airport. And I was kicked off the plane. I was supposed to go to Lyon, but I was taken off the plane at Marseille because I had been sick during the flight. I woke up the next morning, and since I had a bracelet that my jeweler boyfriend had made for me, I found a jewelry shop and showed them my bracelet. The jeweler looked at me with disdain. He thought I had stolen it because it was so fine and large. It looked a bit like one of those huge napkin rings you put on a table. I sold it to pay for my room and a train ticket up to Paris, where I had a scholarship. My mother let me leave without money. I had notes from Bounoure's lectures on Baudelaire in a leather briefcase which I forgot on the airplane. I never got those back. They were my most precious possession. Truly. I thought I had been born to read poetry. And that nothing else could be worth the trouble.

4.

LA: Today I'd like to talk with you about landscapes. What is a landscape for you?

EA: I think the word "landscape" is a cultural word. It's not a land. It's not a place. It's something we have singled out in nature. We've sort of pulled it out of nature, landscape. Which implies that it's important, that we pay attention to it. In general, it's beautiful, but not necessarily. There are more precise terms like "a field" or "a terrain." These are more interesting words. As for the word "landscape," it got big in the nineteenth century with painting. It meant that the subject of the painting wasn't a portrait. Landscape is an important part of place and of terrain.

LA: Would you say you paint landscapes?

EA: If I wanted to be clever, I'd say I paint paintings. But in fact, I wouldn't call what I have in mind a landscape. Since it's not another thing, let's say I have the feeling of a landscape, alright, because I couldn't say: I'm making an abstract painting. There's always a reference to landscape. Maybe because at one time I really loved Monet, and what were later called the impressionists. And then color is space, it's colored space, and a landscape returns you to space. I like landscape paintings; for instance, I like . . . Turner—his are marine landscapes—but before him there was Albrecht Dürer; his pictures have a severity that the impressionists don't. The impressionists projected their love of landscape. There's a sweetness, a kindness toward the landscape.

LA: Is it the sentiment or the sensation of the landscape that interests you?

EA: It's maybe more the sensation than the sentiment. A real landscape is physical. You're inside it. It's very physical, the notion of landscape. In literature, with Lamartine, the lake is a landscape. You see it. But it's not present.

LA: Are you a landscape artist?

EA: Yes, but I've never seen myself as an "artist." Don't laugh. It's a word that disturbs me. I'm not used to it.

LA: How would you define yourself, then? How would you speak about what you do? Is the word "artist" too pretentious?

EA: I have always said "I write" or "I paint." I've never said, "I'm an artist." I find it a difficult term to wear. I don't know why.

LA: Because it maybe implies a kind of loftiness, or superiority over others?

EA: Yes, to be an artist . . . I find we use it far too much. I don't know, it's a term . . .

LA: Do you think everyone can be an artist?

EA: Everyone is in a certain measure. Yes, everyone wants to express something as well as they can. When I undertake to do something, I do it completely. I do it full-time, like I did with writing. Sometimes one thing, sometimes the other; it's already a lot and it's all I did. When I was young, I sometimes helped out with the press, I made cover designs for the books. Sometimes I proofread texts.

LA: Which newspaper did you work at in Beirut?

EA: The only French newspaper in Beirut was *L'Orient-Le Jour*. Dominique Eddé, who became an important writer, was my assistant. That's where she learned newspaper writing. I protected her a lot because she took a long time to write. The boss would say: "This isn't a university; you have to move fast." I'd reply: "Sure, but with Dominique the result is always very good; she takes some time, it's not a big deal." I had five or six young girls like that who were learning to work.

LA: You live with Simone; do you think she has influenced you, or that Simone has been influenced by you, artistically?

EA: I think she has given me a freedom that I had never had before. It's actually a lot. The freedom to do what we did when we did. For example, we said all of a sudden: "Let's go to Paris," and we went to Paris. And also, to be able to write and paint without having to worry about selling something. It's good. Because I was in a new world, a new language. We were in the right place, in San Francisco, it was lively. To see the sunset, things like that. I had interesting friends. We went to New York often; we'd spend weeks there. It was the good life.

LA: And the fact that you were two women in a couple, that didn't cause any problems?

EA: Not at all, no one ever bothered us. Not even in Beirut. I'd even say especially not in Beirut. I think it's because we never paid attention. We didn't think it would pose us problems. No, no problem.

LA: Maybe your love protected you?

EA: I think what protected us was that we did as we pleased, and that included everything. We didn't think about it, we loved each other, that's all.

LA: Artist couples are rare . . . . In fact, it was you who proposed she come to the United States with you.

EA: I told her: "Come see how you like it," and she liked it a lot. It was later on that she began to make sculpture and founded the publishing house. She has always loved literature.

LA: For you, the revelation that you were an artist took place in the United States; for her as well. Was there a sort of simultaneity of artistic birth for the two of you? You gave each other confidence.

EA: There's still a kind of freedom to all points of view in the United States. You can change your life, your occupation, everything. And the country enables that, so it allowed Simone to get out of her family, it really helped her in that sense. She felt less monitored by her mother. It felt right to me, and life kept us very busy. We met interesting and important poets. During the 1960s, I had met those who were writing about the Vietnam War.

Poetry fed into drawing and vice versa. Then drawing took up a lot of space. I wasn't teaching anymore. I was studying. For example, the drawings of Henri Michaux. I experience the same anguish. I live through the same world, but drawing is really so opposite. Drawing is a bit like a sport—the body is more involved—but writing is very tense. It's unbearable. All writers go to physiotherapists; they have cramps. Physically it's a very hard job. Whereas with painting, you move, you look around for your colors, you make gestures. The gesture is very important. It's a world that frees you up more. And then there's an immediate joy. You make a painting, you might spend several hours, it's done. It's the same person. But it's not the same aspect of the person.

LA: Let's talk about philosophy. You're also a philosopher, in your own way. You've pursued studies; you went to the Sorbonne to study philosophy. Notably, you had Gaston Bachelard as a professor. What did he provide you?

EA: The fact that philosophy is not a break with daily life, and that daily life is poetry. This is very important. We think that we owe this to the Anglo-Saxon tradition. We don't know the originality and freedom of Gaston Bachelard's thinking well enough. He was widely read. There was even a cult. Students lined up to get into his classroom. In spite of this, I have the impression that up until now we haven't situated Bachelard or recognized his importance to French thought.

I find his writing to be as extraordinary as the surrealist manifestos. I'd put him on this level. Surrealism is true philosophy as well. But it's a philosophy well ahead of what people considered to be philosophy. For instance, Heidegger said, "The outcome of philosophy is poetry." Surrealism had said this before. Bachelard had said it before. Bachelard had freed up, dusted off the image we had of philosophy as something detached from the world. People like Bachelard rediscovered that in each milieu we are the totality of our life and the totality of the world. It seems facile to say, but it's very, very apt. We are in each second the result of our lives, of our environment, of the history of the world. For me, Bachelard is an exceptional mind in contemporary French thought. We often talk about Deleuze, people who sought to broaden the field of philosophy a bit. Bachelard did this quite naturally.

LA: The experience of reverie and dreams was very important to the philosophical, but also the poetic work of Bachelard.... Has it been important for you?

EA: There is a dream state. When you dream, you rarely know it. But when you wake, you see it, you carry within yourself almost the temperature of the dream, like a warmth of the dream. By "dream," Bachelard almost means a forethought. At times there is a halo around the thought. There's a surface to the thought. There's a little world, and it's very engrossing. Not only the dream as experience, which is interesting because it's like a window, as if the world wasn't big enough; there are also openings to other worlds. Sometimes, when I had nightmares, I'd think to myself: But it's me making up these nightmares. Why are you hurting yourself? You make up experiences too, real experiences like flying. You often have the impression of having flown, like swimming in the river, but parallel to it and not above it. These are, nevertheless, experiences that are physically impossible in a waking state. The mere fact that we dream is amazing.

LA: And to create is to abandon rational thought and abandon yourself to the imagination?

EA: Creation is a form of thinking. It's abandoning a certain world of preoccupations to enter into another. I like the word "make"; the word "create" reminds me too much of religion. I don't know why. We've separated creators from non-creators. And everyone creates, in that sense. Everyone does things that generate the world of philosophy. There's no absolute division. There are different intensities.

I'm astonished by the metaphysical questions that children ask. They have a freedom such that they're able to surprise you with their remarks. We don't record them, fortunately we don't publish them. But that doesn't mean there aren't moments of higher thought. Flashes of illumination. Lately, I have come to the conclusion that, on the level of what we call thinking, everything thinks. I don't know, but it's the feeling that sometimes life is life. If an object exists, it's alive. Otherwise, it wouldn't be there. So, life and thinking go together. There's a whole mystery, a feeling at times that animals think. We say they don't think, even Descartes says that animals are machines . . . but animals think, they make decisions. Before it jumps, a cat looks, gauges the distance; it doesn't fling itself eyes closed into the air. Between a large and a small piece of meat, a dog will pick the large one, so it makes comparisons. Just because they don't think like we do doesn't mean they don't think at all. Everything that is alive thinks, in this sense.

LA: In America you discovered a new light, a beauty in nature. You've known how to talk to flowers since childhood. But on this new continent, you learned to speak to mountains. You wrote a very beautiful book about this experience, called *Journey to Mount Tamalpais*.

EA: America isn't a country, it's a world. It's huge, and historically, an unbelievable energy was unleashed. There has been the best as well as the worst. It's a country where people refashioned their lives. There's a feeling of liberty; everything is possible. It's not false. You can make your life up. In the morning you can pack your bags, move to the next town, and start over. Of course, I don't forget, there's also the genocide of the Native Americans, the problems of Black people, the atom bomb. It's a world with everything. And I love America in a clear way. I see all of it. I still say that in my case, and in the case of millions of people, it has been a liberation, a new world. But that doesn't mean it's the case for everyone or that there's not a price to pay.

People who come to study in France, unfortunately, don't see the natural parts of Europe. They're always in the cities, whereas in America, nature is in everyday life. Here, it's rare for a foreigner to go see the Alps or the Rhône. There's great beauty in Europe. But it's still less wild than America. It's domesticated, tamed. In America, nature is violent and present everywhere. You're never outside of nature.

I first discovered nature on a scale that was barely the hundred kilometers between Beirut and Damascus. The great adventure, for me, was the little train that took twelve hours from Beirut to Damascus. In the United States, wherever you happen to be, you're in an extraordinary natural world. How could you not absorb it? And I've discovered—it's not a "discovery" . . . things happen. I don't know why. The fact that near Berkeley, when I was a professor, there was this mountain, a thousand meters high, which is of an extraordinary beauty—it obsessed me. It became my reference. I was not alone when I looked at it. That's not to say I didn't have friends. But my best friend was the mountain. It took me in, it led the way. It was of such beauty that I observed it continually and it became my companion, as I've told you.

LA: Since then, Etel, you've painted many mountains. What's striking in your different artistic disciplines—drawing, painting, writing, poetry—is the intensity of the present. It's also that you've led a parallel life for decades as a professor, writer, and painter. You showed your paintings in the small gallery of one of your friends. You were esteemed by several of your friends who bought work sometimes. And then all at once, ten years ago, not even . . . international repute. Your paintings are sold worldwide and cost a fortune. So, fame came to you just like that?

EA: I've been asked before what it's like for me to be famous. I heard myself answer: "Lucky that it didn't happen earlier!" Because I've led a tranquil life. By tranquil, I mean I did what interested me. Without pressure, without obligations. Success creates obligations, closes you in. I didn't have that experience. The new recognition is a coincidence.

Thanks to my friends, I never felt like I was working in a vacuum. I never thought that I would have work in big galleries either; it wasn't a dream. I showed once in a real professional gallery in Beirut, but only twice in Paris, and in America in small galleries. Mostly I had painter friends, I had a milieu. There are many painters who have never been recognized in history, who kept at it because they had a milieu. We showed amongst ourselves. When I sold a small canvas for a hundred dollars, I was happy. I didn't pay gallerists; they were friends. And then in 2011, a gallerist in Beirut, who also has a gallery in Hamburg, Andrée Sfeir-Semler, told me she wanted to give me a show, for cultural reasons, with another person who worked in sculpture. And two months later, Andrée told me: "You know, the other person who was going to show her sculptures is sick, her daughter doesn't want her to do the show. You can show at my gallery. I'll find someone else, but it will be an ordinary commercial exhibition." I hesitated, then accepted. It happened that Hans Ulrich Obrist had seen a painting of mine and wanted to meet me. When he learned I was having a show in Beirut, he sent Carolyn Christov-Bakargiev, who was planning Documenta 13 for the year 2012. Carolyn arrived—without the gallery knowing—she came to speak with me and told me she was in charge of Documenta. She invited me to breakfast with her at the hotel the next morning. I went and she proposed that I exhibit at Documenta. I was stunned. She said kindly, "You don't want to?" because I wasn't answering! I said: "Yes!" but I was scared, it was a new world, and a lot of work! That's how it began. Once you're in Documenta, it brings you attention. That's how it happens. And since then, I've had a lot of work. It has tired me out.

LA: Painting is tiring?

FA: After a certain age everything is tiring, a bit tiring. Before that you don't think about it, but I worked a lot because the galleries wanted paintings and I was invested, after all! So, I've made a lot of money and I can't even spend it. I look for ways to spend it: I don't go out; I barely go to the movies . . . . It's a kind of irony to make a bunch of money without knowing how to spend it.

LA: It should be noted that Documenta is the largest contemporary art fair in the world.

EA: And really, the people in charge there make it their business to ensure that it's exceptional . . .

LA: And to find new talents, like yourself.

EA: And then at the time of Documenta, there were few painters working in oils or acrylics. There were lots of assemblages and installations. But very few of what were called "traditional paintings," at least of that size. There was an Ethiopian painter from America, very famous, but that's it; and an American who made an immense airplane that was twenty meters long. In an enormous room, they'd put all my little paintings, and it turned out these little paintings held up . . . . It must have struck people. There was a tension in each one which made it not seem small. It called attention to itself. And we mustn't forget that painting, as opposed to poetry, is a market. These are objects that can be sold, so galleries look for new people they can launch now, like products. I think that if there are no more galleries, eventually painters will give up. Many will stop work. There must be galleries, since painting is no longer the business of nobility—with murals and frescoes— it's become a bourgeois endeavor; the audience is bourgeois. But it's also big business. Galleries require you to produce. Now, I've stopped; for a year now I've been working much less because I worked too much for three or four years.

It was a whirlwind because I had four galleries. And each one watches the others: "What? You gave him paintings, but not me?" So, I had to even things out. Since then, I've continued to work; I just had a show. But it's much less all the same. It's fatigue; it's my age. I'm very lucky to be able to work at my age, ninety-three years old, it's terrific. And I feel it, it's difficult to walk, but it doesn't tire me out to paint. It's restful for me sometimes.

It's more tiring for me to write. And the worst is to reply to email, because the email comes from all over the world! It makes your head go in all directions. After four of them, my day is over.

You write to New York; you write to Paris. You write I don't know where. It's a terrifying fatigue. I'd rather make a painting than respond to two emails.

5.

LA: How are you feeling, Etel?

EA: It's a bore to live life between two chairs. I want to leave, and I said this to my doctor.

LA: Leave?

EA: Yes, leave. He told me: "But you're more lucid than most of my patients. I can't get rid of you. It's impossible. You need to walk to the kitchen and back three times per day. That gives you exercise, and you'll be better."

LA: What a marvelous doctor!

EA: He told me I had to . . . had to . . .

LA: Continue living?

EA: Yes, that's it. So, I wondered what I could still do. I can draw anyway.

LA: That's already a lot, that's huge.

EA: And drawing with black ink on white canvases is nice because the contrast is strong. I buy Japanese inks. They're magnificent. Chinese and Japanese inks on white canvases—it's very lively.

LA: Yes, because you've drawn a lot on paper, but on canvas, with black ink?

EA: An ordinary canvas, small like that. I'll show you, it's very powerful. It's beautiful.

LA: Does your hand guide you, or is the drawing you're going to make in your head already?

EA: No, I place a bottle and I draw it. It's very beautiful, black on a strong white. And it makes you want to keep going, to redo.

LA: And so, to live; to live here in Paris.

EA: Luckily, my doctor loves the drawings.

LA: So, you're going to keep drawing?

EA: I'm deeply bored. I don't sleep. It's because I'm not tired enough to sleep, and it's not easy to be in a wheelchair. I can't go to the Luxembourg gardens anymore. I don't do it because you freeze to death on these chairs when you're not moving, when you're doing nothing. And then it's not easy to get to the elevator either, to get down the stairs. I can go to Brittany, but it's difficult to take the train. They have to carry you into the train car. There are people there to help, but still. There are good doctors in Erquy, but no clinic. When the warm weather comes, I'll go. At the apartment there, you're facing the sea. And it's beautiful. It's two hours from Paris, it's nothing. Two hours and a ten-minute taxi—it's no big deal. And to be constantly in front of the horizon, by the end of a week, you forget about solid land and the countryside. You habituate. It's very nice. Brittany is beautiful. I've discovered something that really struck me: beaches are architectures. Truly, each beach . . . nature has created an architecture, and it's great, because you realize the richness of this beauty. There's a lovely sand beach at Sables-d'Or, close to Erquy. But each of these beaches is beautiful because each has its personality.

LA: When you say that each beach has its architecture, is it the ocean that has built the architecture of the beach?

EA: Yes, it's the ocean, the forces of nature. In Brittany there's the forest of Brocéliande. Everyone from the Round Table comes from this place, north of Quimper. It's in the center of Brittany, two hours from where I am. Brittany makes me think of Lebanon, at times. What's beautiful in Lebanon is the color. There's a pink particular to that part of the world. There's a pink color in the villages. You sit in a village, and you see pink hillsides. And the earth, the limestone. The limestone is vitrified. It's a reflective material, like glass, and it's very beautiful. Or the pink granite; columns of pink granite. Greek columns are white, not pink. But pink granite, it's like sequins, it's very beautiful. And in Lebanon it is this pink that is beautiful. There's a famous hotel, the Saint-Georges, and when you sit on the terrace, you see the salt marshes all pink, from the early afternoon until night. There are landscapes . . . for a small country, it's beautiful. There's a great deal of beauty for a small area, contrary to what people say.

LA: You are still Lebanese; do you still feel yourself to be Lebanese?

EA: Yes, I still feel Lebanese because they make so many blunders; they won't let you forget about them. It's wars, crimes, troubles. My family history haunts me. The upbringing my mother gave me, as well. She said there were only three jobs for a woman: the first was to be a servant, the second was prostitution, and the third was to gather dried grapes. That was all you could do to earn a living. My mother was always afraid to grow old, to not be pretty and go back to living in poverty, since she'd been orphaned very early and was practically living in the street when she married my father. They had some years of being rich, but she never really felt like it since she had this terror of returning to poverty. The good part was that we weren't pretentious, we weren't bourgeois, and we valued things. Today in America, I've seen children receive an entire room full of Christmas gifts; they've barely opened the package before they throw it away. They don't even look to see what's inside. We didn't have this kind of experience. Even if we ate well, my mother would say: "There, we've had a good week . . . " I saw incredible things. For example, the Greek women who gossiped among friends; they told each other everything they did. They'd say: "I met a guy yesterday; he gave me such and such an amount and I bought silk stockings." Everything had value. In

Beirut, we had no telephone. My mother would say: "Ah those people are rich, imagine, they have a telephone at home." Taking a taxi . . . when I'd take one without telling, when I'd begun to work, I felt like a wife cheating on her husband. I was cheating on my parents. I took taxis in secret. It was an interesting feeling. There was no music, but there would be funeral processions passing in the street with drumming and carrying on, and it was like a concert for us at the time. We had a gramophone and I thought there was a little lady inside who sang. There was an innocence, a naivete that I miss. I don't find people who can be truly amazed . . . or who still believe in impossible things. There are no more innocent people. The world is cunning. Innocence is a bit like poetry. It's in poetry that we search . . . even poetry we call sophisticated—Apollinaire for example—there's a freshness, an astonishment, and that's beautiful. Luckily poetry exists. I must have been twenty years old when I first wrote a book, which was never published, because it's still in the drawer. I didn't even know publishers existed. I remember there was a writer in Paris named Thierry Maulnier, and I had read something of his that had struck me. I sent him a letter and I put "Thierry Maulnier, Paris." I thought everyone must know him, that they would give him my letter. He didn't receive it and I came back to the office and the director made fun of me. "You don't send a letter like that, with no address." I didn't know there were addresses. I emancipated myself in wartime Beirut. There are wars that destroy countries and there are others that practically create them. And the Second World War brought entire armies through here. For instance, it was the first time I saw Australians and New Zealanders, they were a foot taller than everyone in town. Beirut got rich then.

I went to work at the army commissariat, and the first day, the officer I worked for told me to climb on the table to reach some file boxes. So, I stood up to pull the files down, he lifted up my skirt, and I toppled over, there was a loud noise . . . . The director of the office, who was the father of a student in my school, called me and asked what had happened. I replied: "Sergeant Huguez lifted my skirt." He tells me: "Okay, go back home and ask your mother to come see me." And he says to her: "Madame, when you have such a young and naive child, you cannot send her to a military office. I can't monitor my officers . . . . If you want her to work, she has to find a civil office . . ." That's how I was assigned to the Press Bureau.

LA: What a disgrace, for the soldier . . .

EA: Yeah, but the guy from the office said: "My hands are tied." He didn't say a word to the sergeant; he asked my mother to send me to work somewhere else.

LA: That didn't shock you at the time? Was it normal?

EA: Eh, no, we weren't shocked by male behavior towards women. It was like the guy who bankrupted my father so he could make a marriage proposal to my mother. It was after the Second World War that things shifted. They began to shift in Europe, in the English-speaking world. Otherwise, women weren't heard. They weren't written about; they weren't spoken of. They were told, "Just sit there and look pretty." Even later, when the Syrians controlled Lebanon, there were officers or soldiers who tried to abuse girls. And certain women who lived with powerful men went to Damascus to see Hafez al-Assad, to tell him: "Your soldiers are conducting themselves badly." He answered: "Collect your daughters. Keep them at home, so they don't get out."

The question of women remains unresolved to this day, and we must be careful. Even me, for example: when I wrote a novel about the Lebanese civil war, the phalangists called the paper where I worked and said: "If we see Etel's byline in the paper, it won't be distributed." That meant in Achrafieh, the truly Francophone district. The paper's director called me to his office and said he was sorry and asked me to resign, because we had to sell newspapers, and unless I did so they would never be sold in Achrafieh. His voice got friendly all of a sudden and he said in a simpering tone: "And anyway, who asked you to write what you think?" He told me, as if it were advice: "See what a pickle it gets you in." I replied, "But really, I was getting paid to write what I thought." When I had first arrived at the paper, they had told me: "No politics here, you're an art critic." You don't opine, you only write descriptions. But it's not really so fun to be an art critic. I wrote what I thought. I criticized tons of bad work. One day, some people had bought a painting by a bad painter in a gallery. They were so proud of this that they tacked up their calling card next to the red dot, and I wrote in my review, "Why not just put their photo?" There was an entertainment section, written by some young women, and in this section, the gossip column reported the opposite of what I wrote. They said this was a major painter. So, I went to see the editor and he asked me, "Are these girls preventing you from writing what you want?" I said no. "So why would you try to stop them from writing what they want?" He refused to get involved.

Existence is incredible and sometimes takes an accidental turn. My life turned upside down because of a simple remark. One day, in California, I was walking in the university garden, along a path lined with roses—there were nothing but roses at the college— and there, a woman professor stops me and says: "Are you the new professor?" I answered yes. "What do you teach?" I said philosophy of art. She was head of the art department. Then she asks me: "Do you paint?" I said no. "How can you teach about painting if you have never tried?" Spontaneously, I answered her: "My mother said I was clumsy." She looked at me and said, "And you believed her?" This freed my hands. Right away. This remark, and the way she looked at me. And the calling into question, too, released me. She told me: "Come to my department," and I went; she gave me paper and pastels and I scribbled. She told me, "Your mind is trained, you don't need classes." She left the college, and she gave seminars at her own house. She would let her students paint, and at the end of the afternoon they would discuss among themselves and with her. This was her method; there were no more of the old-style courses. She created a center that still exists to this day. "You cannot teach art; you must let people work." She said things like this, and several of her students made a book of what she taught. Her name was Ann O'Hanlon. Her husband was a sculptor, she was a painter and had become one thanks to what Roosevelt had put into place, the WPA (Works Progress Administration). For example, she had been to Kentucky, where she learned to paint murals, which were paid for by the state. Roosevelt created jobs, what Biden is calling "build back." But it's not the same. Roosevelt wasn't giving people money. He created jobs: art schools, for instance. In San Francisco, they had public art made. That's how he got America back on its feet, with work.

What she did is marvelous because the students listen to one another; they're much more interested in each other than in the teacher. As soon as one of them gets up, everyone listens attentively. But the remark, the timing is another notion of time. We speak a lot about time, but not enough about the importance of timing. Some people miss out on their lives because of poor timing. They haven't said the right thing at the right moment, or they said the wrong thing at the wrong moment. Timing: there are moments like that where you think: ah, if only I'd jumped on it. It's a good word in English. And it was that remark by Ann O'Hanlon that brought me to the art department the next day and got me to work.

LA: Without your teacher you would never have become a painter?

EA: I had first been a teacher myself at the college, and I had already noticed the extent to which, when a student said something, everyone listened, everyone was encouraged. They respected each other, mutually. I remember this moment, during the Vietnam war, we were discussing courage and I told the students: "We have a young man here, David. David, what do you think of courage?" He stood and replied: "I don't know what courage is. I am a coward because I wouldn't be sent to Vietnam. I want to avoid fighting, so if I am in LA today, it's because I said I was ill and went to the infirmary, and that's how I avoided fighting." We were all rapt; it was a moment of extraordinary truth to hear this young man say: "I was not courageous, and I stand by it." I've never forgotten this moment. This boy who stood up—there are moments like that, unforgettable. Another unforgettable moment in my life was in Berkeley. There was a tradition over there of great geniuses; many of the genius minds of the era, teaching, giving lectures and conferences for free to the public. So, a young American woman told me to go hear Taylor, the inventor of the atom bomb. And Taylor gave a very bleak lecture. But during his talk, he recited by heart from beginning to end the book of Omar Khayyam. Every three or four sentences, he recited a poem by heart. And it was gripping to hear, like a fist pounding the table, these poems that came back in a disheartened, sad tone, by this true genius. He recited it all by heart. Of all the poetry sessions I've attended, this was the most powerful. It was marvelous. It's this, this innocence, which is missing. He went to the trouble of knowing these poems by heart and then he found the suitable moment . . . . It gives me chills, to this day. It was incredible. They happen, unforgettable moments like this one. Related to the atomic bomb, to death and to poetry . . . and to structural pessimism. Since then, I have never believed in "truth" in the naïve sense of the word.

LA: What definition would you give of "truth?"

EA: I think henceforth it's an indefensible concept. Philosophy is not the search for truth. Philosophy is a construction, a mental architecture. Big theories are mental constructions, plausible or fitting, or that open doors to further research, but we no longer speak of . . . after Foucault and Deleuze, we don't speak of truth anymore. We speak of propositions or else of momentary, limited truths. But of truth in the absolute sense . . . there's something else, though: experience, lived experience which is a form of truth. We can talk about it another time. It's interesting.

6.

LA: What is "beauty" for you, Etel?

EA: So, it's very simple. We're going to start at the beginning. Last October, I got a note from a curator at Tate Modern in London. His name is Achim Borchardt-Hume; he has lots of friends all over the world. I had never met him, but he'd seen something somewhere that I said about Cézanne. And he said to me: "We're putting on the first ever retrospective of Cézanne in England." I told him: "I hope you're going to put *The Gardener Vallier* in this show." He asked me why, adding that he doesn't think it will be included, and I replied that for me, it's the most important of Cézanne's paintings, and I described it for him. The gardener has long, slender legs. He's seated in the entryway of Cézanne's studio. He's not alone; he's a true philosopher. The director of the Tate asked me to keep talking about Cézanne, and I told him that we've made him into a classic, but that in reality a Cézanne painting is organized chaos. For me, this particular painting of his embodies beauty. If we reproduce a painting of Cézanne's in the world such as it exists around us, in our everyday space, nothing makes sense. The tablecloths are vertical, the little pieces of china are going to break, the apples will roll, it's a shambles. On my

75

table I happened to find a book by Deleuze, a series of lectures. I looked at it . . . and I found it boring. To me, Deleuze didn't say anything interesting about Cézanne. The piece that interested me most was by Pierre Klossowski, who I consider a great mind. He far surpasses his brother, the painter Balthus. These are lectures on Nietzsche. Nietzsche said, "God is dead. Therefore, man is dead." And I thought: and the world—the material world—is doubtless dead. It made me think.

You're asking me about beauty. Beauty is the bouquet of flowers that Yvon Lambert gave me, a little while back. I met him recently; he's not an old friend, but he always brings flowers that smell very strong and very good. His favorite flower is the peony. He showed up with a bouquet; there was a peony of a red color I had never before seen in reality. And I thought it was a rose. I thought: but roses don't have this sort of very strong pigmentation. What is color? And I realized suddenly that color was the manifestation of the will to power of matter. Nothing in the world is as strong as the red of this peony that has just come into my existence, and it's something to reflect upon.

In my book on Mount Tamalpais, I talk about Cézanne and Hokusai, and about their mountains. Beauty is also a revelation. At the time when man first walked on the moon, I was very struck by all this movement towards the moon and wondered why earthlings want to go up in space. Maybe they go in search of a new revelation. I thought: revelation is indivisible. For me, revelation is the moment where, all at once, a human being, someone, discovers the divine within him. These are fleeting things. Revelation is really the *eternal return* of Nietzsche, but I thought that Nietzsche was old and very tired when he spoke about eternal return. He said the world would repeat itself, exactly as it is. Now, the material world cannot repeat itself identically. Because we're already in a different time, and time is part of the world. It happens to all of us: we have an idea, and it disappears before it concludes. And we forget it for good. So, I found, or thought I found, a plausible definition of *eternal return,* which had long tormented me. The two important intuitions were made possible by the lockdown. I've been in a wheelchair for two years now. So what? There you go, I'm bound to think.

What is missing in French culture? All cultures we know of contain a dogmatic part, severe and hard, but they also have a certain mysticism, which doesn't exist structurally in French culture. Where and how did that begin? I've reasoned that in the 17ᵗʰ century, you had Pascal and Descartes, and France made a choice, because of the Jesuits and perhaps also because Pascal's *Pensées* were really poetry. They are thoughts that serve as poetry. And France did not follow this path; it chose a certain simplistic idea of Descartes': "I think, hence I am"; but I eat, hence I am, also; I don't see why not . . . something happened during the 17th century to silence Pascal. Besides, they blacklisted him, and the blacklist existed until not that long ago. I recall when I was hired as a professor, they told me: "We want a French professor, we don't want a philosophy professor this year." I agreed, I needed a salary; I did a course on French culture, and I put *Nausea* by Sartre on the syllabus. Since it was a Catholic college, the director told me: "We have to ask the college priests for permission from the archbishop. You must submit your list of texts." I found that funny; I asked if there was still a blacklist and he replied that yes, there was. He came back from the archbishop and told me the archbishop was very cross. "You put Sartre in there"—this was in 1958—"and Sartre is blacklisted for everything he has written and for everything he will ever write." "You mean to say he cannot be saved?" "No, he will never change, he's blacklisted forever." So, I said: "I can't teach a course on contemporary thought without including a book by Sartre." And he responded: "Wait a bit." I had also put *The Red and the Black* by Stendhal on the syllabus. The director told the archbishop: "*The Red and the Black* is a good cheese." There was, in fact, a cheesemaker in the neighborhood called Le Rouge et le Noir. That reassured the archbishop. He said: "Okay, for this year I'll allow Stendhal and Sartre as well."

7.

LA: What does it mean, for you, to "think?"

EA: What it means to think . . . I don't know, "thought" is something our brain secretes. It's a power of the mind, we don't really know what it is.

LA: But when you write, Etel, do you think? When you paint, are you thinking?

EA: When I paint, I don't believe so. Unless it's so impulsive that I'm unaware. When you write it seems more obvious. I don't know if you're thinking also. It's a current, a river you follow. I don't know. Recently, for example in certain poems, I've wondered. I asked myself why we think so little about memory in contemporary thought, even as we are at the very moment of a pandemic; I don't comprehend how, philosophically, this is not at the center of our thinking. Unfortunately, I have the time, but I can't read, it tires me to read.

LA: You say that when you paint, you're not thinking. So, what is happening?

EA: I don't know if you call it a "thought." For instance, when I put two colors together: there's a situation and I must proceed. I have to continue the painting. And I search, I look at the paints and I look for what I call the "following color." I don't call that a "thought." Maybe it is a thought anyway? I don't know.

LA: And what is that, the "following color"?

EA: It's a color that will create a new situation. And something in me will judge if it works or if it doesn't work, and where to go. I call all of these decisions. Maybe it's thoughts. As you say, what is it to think? These are certainly thoughts of the moment, or reflections. But I don't linger on them. The thing in itself doesn't interest me. I want to move forward. Let's go. Painting is interesting; it's another world.

LA: You say "let's go," but where do we go, then, with painting?

EA: With painting, you're in a parallel world, different, like with music. There are worlds and there are worlds. There are realities and realities.

LA: That we can attain only by thought or by the artistic act? To go toward these other worlds. How do we go there?

EA: We go there probably by chance. It's as if someone suddenly opened a door for you. You take a first step, and you decide whether or not to stay. I don't know.

LA: A first step toward what?

EA: Toward the thing that has appeared or will appear. You don't know. If you knew, you wouldn't keep going. You don't know. It's good to admit you don't know. Me, one day, in the middle of teaching, my students asked me: "Do you believe in God?" I heard myself reply yes, but I don't know what it means. We don't know what it is. We know approximately. I mean, we know enough to manipulate things we call knowledge, to advance, to live from day to day, but we don't know. You see, I don't know.

LA: We don't know, but we keep going, always toward the unknown. We go double-quick, toward what we don't know. Everyone doesn't go, I mean not everyone, but you do.

EA: Because to live is to be launched into what we call life. There are poets, for instance Baudelaire or Rimbaud, whose texts seem to lead you along; they are there, and you chase after them. I thought of a short passage from Rimbaud that says "[...] we are committed to the discovery of divine light." It's a poem called "Farewell," I believe.

LA: And today, to the question of God, if I ask you like the students asked you decades ago, what would you say?

EA: If I believe in God? I believe more in the divine than in God. Because I have had the experience of sensing the divine, which points to this, and which escaped me at the very moment it took place.

LA: When did you experience it?

EA: Some years ago, I think. But there are things like this. For example, there have been moments where a painting has provoked a feeling that went beyond the ordinary. Or even landscapes do this, sometimes. There are places in the world. And it's not necessarily spectacular.

LA: And so, what happens at that moment?

EA: Nothing lasting occurs. It's always very quick. I don't know.

LA: It's like a flash. Like lightning?

EA: Even the moment when you meet someone: we call it love at first sight, and it is a lightning strike. It's a thing that has struck you and is gone, it doesn't last.

LA: Love at first sight doesn't last? Love at first sight can endure, no?

EA: No, the consequences can last. But the thing itself, it's like lightning in winter, it crosses the sky. Music does this.

LA: And when you speak about a decision while you are painting, what type of decision is it?

EA: You don't know where the decision comes from. It can come from the object. For instance, you have ten paint colors and all of a sudden, one of them jumps out at you. You don't know. You truly don't know. But there's the idea of a path. Whether you follow or make it up, it amounts to the same thing.

LA: And you know when a painting is finished.

EA: It's very strange, but a painting is finished because . . . there's a particular feeling that a thing is done, that something more would spoil what you have.

LA: This is a thing you know?

EA: You feel it. It's the word "end."

LA: For the poem too?

EA: The poem too, the novel too. You feel that to touch it will commit you—maybe you're tired—and it will commit you more than you want at that moment, because you shift one thing and then everything else shifts too. If you're at that point, it means the painting is finished.

LA: You're not like certain painters who sometimes revisit very old paintings. Retouching isn't your strong suit?

EA: It depends on their method of working. I rarely revisit. It's done, it's done, it doesn't interest me anymore.

LA: It's behind you? Why do you say, "it no longer interests me"?

EA: Painting is another world from writing.

LA: You find the same pleasure in the two, or the same satisfaction, or the same desire?

EA: You need to know that it's another world. Otherwise, you wouldn't go. It's astonishing, you do a thing you don't know. Perhaps it's so that you can know what it is that you continue to paint. You don't know. But it's instinctive. Children like to paint, it soothes them, they need to paint.

LA: And you, do you also need to paint?

EA: If I have done it, it's because I needed to return to it. Even now that I can't write, that I can't read, I can draw. The trace, to leave traces, must be very vital, it must be a very deep-seated need within us. We see it in the rock paintings of the person who drew a cow at Lascaux; she had a particular impulse, a particular need.

8.

LA: What's new today, Etel?

EA: Oh, lots of things. Simone went to Erquy, she bought the restaurant, because she's wanted to turn it into her studio for a long time now. She wants a place to work, and there's a room downstairs, in the restaurant. The kitchen is a real room. We're going there in early June, and I hope to spend two or three months there. Usually, I spend two good months there.

LA: And what do you do there?

EA: I don't do anything; I draw a bit. I really like to draw.

LA: You look at the sea in Erquy?

EA: In Erquy I don't do anything; I sit, I watch the sea, and I eat ice cream. Because it's summer and that's all. It's not bad.

LA: What does that mean, "do nothing," for you, Etel?

EA: It's nice to do nothing, it's not difficult. I bought headphones but I find them uncomfortable, and I will put them in if I want to listen to music. But it's not a natural sound, it's not beautiful. It's wrong. On the other hand, I don't require anything to draw. I do one or two drawings first thing in the morning when I wake up. It entertains me. I've got to try this black against the white of the canvas. It's very beautiful, you see. Every morning I have a date with the black, but it's a lively black. I don't like black so much, but this is a Japanese black. I prefer to buy it on the rue de Pont-Louis-Philippe, and it's pleasant, this black is vibrant, it's not depressing.

LA: What does that mean, a "depressing" color?

EA: There are depressing combinations that sometimes pull you down. But this one, no.

LA: Still, they say your painting is very joyful. Do you agree with this psychological term?

EA: It's possible. It is clear, it's not muddy; it's sharp enough. It's maybe joyful, but they say you feel poetry in my paintings. It's possible. Why not, when it gets down to it.

LA: We can't say that you have always used bright colors. In front of me I have a painting of yours—I don't know from when—but the background of the painting is dark green, and in the center there are colored shapes that are quite dark, too.

EA: I don't remember much of what I've already done. It was Mallarmé who said he was anxious in front of a blank page; in fact, each day is a blank page. You don't know.

LA: So, it's better not to remember what you've done?

EA: No, I don't really like to. And there's a feeling of discovery when I work. Let's see what the result will be. It sustains you while you work. Let's see; we don't know ahead of time. We'll find out. Each book is an adventure. We don't know where we're going.

LA: And each painting is a new beginning?

EA: Yes, each painting, like each poem, like everything you do, is a new beginning. Besides, it's this curiosity that leads us, that gives us the energy to continue. We're going to see how this turns out. We don't know.

LA: Does age bring a feeling of risk?

EA: Age is an additional problem. You know, one learns very little. You think that with time and age one learns, but it's not true. When you learn, it's always too late. You don't really learn, and fortunately, because you'd lead your life like a homework assignment to be completed.

LA: Simone wrote a book that's called *Etel Adnan: Painting as Pure Energy*.

EA: Yes, she says my painting is pure energy. It's probably because she sees me sitting here working. What we call "being alive," it is having energy; that's it, to be alive. You don't know what you're going to do and then the pleasure of discovery, even the impact of a line—it's already a discovery. We discover the day-to-day.

LA: The last time I saw you paint I had the impression that you were just discovering what it means to paint, even though you've been painting for decades now.

EA: It's true, I don't know. It remains a mystery. Otherwise, I wouldn't do it anymore. I believe it stays a mystery, and the feeling of mystery draws us on, gives us what others would call the "required energy."

LA: And do you think that with age, just as there was the Picasso of the last moments or the Matisse of the last moments—what's called the final work—do you think there's a greater risk taken?

EA: It's possible. For the last drawings I've been doing, you know, I have the inkwells, the two pomegranates, and that's it. I've done about fifty drawings. It hasn't gotten old for me. Picasso, he came to his end with women. These tortured women he painted—he deformed them, hid their faces, and it's frightening. Did he hate them? Fear them? Maybe his mother had power over him, I don't know, but there's a problem with Picasso and women, and in the end, he's eaten up by them. They become these caverns that he fears.

LA: Is your painting a woman's painting, Etel, or is this question completely stupid?

EA: I don't know. If we decide that women are "soft power," then it's certainly a kind of painting that soothes, that is tranquil.

LA: We might say your painting soothes.

EA: That depends. There's an angular side to the squares, the straight lines. It's not necessarily soothing. But there's an innate search for balance, and balance is soothing. I believe in beauty. Soothing is part of beauty. And why not?

LA: For the recent Venice Architecture Biennale, you made a new cycle of olive trees with Hala Wardé for the Lebanese pavilion.

EA: Yes, Hala Wardé is an architect and she wanted to take part in the architecture Biennale. One day, Jean Frémon gave me some large octagonal canvases. I said: "But Jean, what am I going to do with these?" He answered: "You'll find something." And looking at them, I thought: I'm going to draw trees. The trees fit into the curves, and in all I made sixteen paintings. As soon as they were finished, Simone and Hans Ulrich Obrist said spontaneously: "We must not separate them." And I said yes. When Hala Wardé saw them, she said: "I'm going to borrow them and propose a way to put them up." Jean came to get them. He managed to find a woman who is the sister of a banker in Beirut. She bought them all. I told her: "I don't want to separate them," and she reassured me: "No, I promise you, we won't separate them." She gave them to the Musée d'Art Moderne, on the avenue d'Iéna, with the condition that they are not separated. But meanwhile, I latched on to the idea that we should revive the growing of olive trees on both sides of the Mediterranean. And we created an association to unite as many as possible of the legends surrounding the olive tree. For example, there's an olive grove north of Beirut, and the village farmers believe that when the bird brought the olive branch to Noah, it took it from this place.

The king of Morocco, the grandfather of the one today, the papa of Hassan II (who was a good man), lived under Vichy rule, so the Germans came and asked him for a list of Jewish citizens of Morocco. He refused: "No, I can't give them to you. They are my subjects, like the others." They exiled him to Madagascar for daring to say no. At the end of his stay there, at the end of the war, he was repatriated. They let him back in and he asked, to celebrate his return, that each ten-year-old Moroccan child plant an olive tree in commemoration. And the children did it. I also read in Herodotus that Thales, who was Phoenician, lived in the south in Miletus. And Thales had long foreseen a year when the olive harvest would be very abundant, so he bought all the presses in the town so that when the harvest came, they would be rented from him; and he said: "Just because I am a scholar, doesn't mean I'm not a businessman." It's a good story: Thales made money buying olive presses. But the important thing is that we continue to plant olive trees in the Mediterranean and in Lebanon, especially around the Mediterranean. In Sardinia there are a lot. Sardinia had the biggest Phoenician trading post, by Cagliari, and it's covered in olive trees. But the most beautiful is Delphi, because in

Delphi there's a cultural center up above. And when you sit there, you look all the way to the sea and the entire hill is covered in olive trees. No houses, nothing. And it looks like the Mediterranean is gray because of the olive trees.

LA: And why don't you want your olive trees to be separated? Because they form a family, for you? The olive tree is a tree from your childhood, no?

EA: Olive oil was important at the table. We'd put a bit of olive oil on everything. You put a dash of vinegar with olive oil, the flavor is there. When we weren't feeling good, they'd put warm olive oil on our foreheads. It's a beneficial oil that was used as a medicine. It's very important.

LA: Can you speak to trees, Etel?

EA: Speak to trees, not much, no, but I sense that they are listening. When you put music on for them. When you get back from a trip and you're in the garden or in the house, they fare better. They feel; they communicate with one another underground. Trees are very beautiful. It's the idea that everything is alive, that it's all connected. And that they hear us and need us.

LA: And that we need them, as well.

EA: Yes, but in the centuries to come, we will rediscover a belonging among all things. We've become too separated. Never could we have imagined such brutality. We're cruel. We put nails into the trees. We put electrical wires; it exhausts the tree. Fortunately, there are many young people the world over, especially in Europe and America, fighting to protect nature. We've got to return to the bicycle. For example: require young people to use bicycles from such and such a time of day to another; they do it a great deal already. The pandemic has proven that when the state takes an urgent measure, people listen. So, we're going to have to, I won't say ban the automobile, but require that we not use it as much as possible. Look, China is a terrible ecological disaster. In Beijing, you can't breathe. In Mao's time, everyone could breathe and was on a bicycle. And India is polluting at full steam. We're going to shift; the world will shift.

LA: You think the pandemic will contribute to the acceleration of changes in life and decisions on the climate?

EA: Yes, indirectly. If only by proving that it's possible to supervise, to require. Because pollution is as grave for our health as the virus.

9.

LA: I'd like for us to talk about Simone and you, and about your story. How did it begin?

EA: Simone, I've said, began making sculpture in America. I saw her holding some eggplants one day and I thought: She's a sculptor. She had such a grasp of these objects. There was a colleague in the neighborhood who hosted classes. She very quickly found things to do. For example, she made centaurs and female characters right away. It's natural for her, it entertains her. There's a mix of imagination, play, and work that suits her. Neither one of us had a gallery, but we had a friend who made ceramic sculptures, his wife was a great potter, they had a kiln and a Japanese house, so we went to their place all the time. One day, they exhibited Simone's work and mine in their studio. It was always the same people who came, and that lasted for years. We showed for years at friends' places. Why not? And voilà. It's only lately that she has had a show at MoMA, the MoMA outside of Manhattan, in Queens, and it drew a lot of people. She's had very good reviews and now everyone wants to show her.

LA: Are you an artistic and a romantic couple?

EA: We have known each other for a very long time. Since 1972. We don't work together artistically, but we certainly have an influence on one another, even if it isn't conscious. We met in Beirut. I had returned from the United States because I had a bad back and the doctor had ordered me to come every day for rehab for six months, in order to avoid a third back surgery. This was a surgeon who had forsworn back operations. Simone was already a painter; she had started painting with a friend of hers who was a good painter. One day, she invited me to come work in her studio in Beirut. I was working for a newspaper, and she'd come to pick me up during work hours—she didn't care. I couldn't get work done anymore, but I managed to hang on to my job. She had a little Mini Cooper and we often went for drives in the desert, and one day she told me: "You don't need to go back to work. You should be doing more of what you want to do," and I thought: she might be right! She came with me to America. I was still a professor, so they were expecting me . . .

LA: What are the landscapes that live within you today, Etel? The landscapes that stay with you?

EA: I've never thought about landscapes in California. Maybe you need to go to Maine to have sudden glimpses that transport you. But California is mostly spaces, it's open. I wouldn't say . . . around Paris, there aren't any! As soon as you stop in front of something, it escapes you. What is a landscape? There's a gesture behind the word "landscape." Look! Voilà. Landscape is this. We don't talk about the urban landscape. Baudelaire speaks of the urban landscape. Baudelaire loved the city of Paris, practically the way other people love nature. It was a new nature for him. He also saw the destruction. He was a contemporary of Haussmann and he witnessed the destruction of a Paris he was fond of, just as we saw the destruction of Les Halles. He loved the Luxembourg gardens and walked there often. In fact, he witnessed the transformation of what later came to be called Saint-Germain—that was his neighborhood.

LA: What did Saint-Germain look like when you got there?

EA: At that time, in 1949, there was the Flore and Les Deux Magots. There was Le Relais Saint-Germain, Le Royal Saint-Germain. There was the Café Saint-Germain at the corner of the rue des Saints-Pères and the boulevard. There was a restaurant that served blueberry tarts; I remember I often went there.

LA: How did you succeed in integrating yourself into the local scene? You didn't know anyone when you arrived?

EA: No, I knew absolutely no one. My friends lived by the Métro Château d'Eau. I didn't have a dime . . . I lived far out, in the university housing, it was a desert. Though there were plenty of students in the residence halls that I chatted with.

LA: You didn't feel lonely?

EA: All told, yes. But I've never used that word. I lived much of my life, as they say, day to day, in the moment. Paris was an immense discovery, when you came from the Beirut of that era, where there were no radios or telephones in the houses. I remember finding the crosswalks very beautiful. I was at the Place de l'Opéra in front of the Café de Paris and I crossed several times diagonally, and the policeman stopped me and said, "Why are you walking this way?" I answered him: "Because it's beautiful."

Paris was a tremendous thing. In the evening I'd go visit friends, and with the youthful—and cruel, besides—insouciance of young people, I'd forget the time of the last train. I'd walk home from Strasbourg-Saint-Denis to the university housing. I was never frightened. There were sinister parts; the end of the boulevard Saint-Michel is not a cheerful place. I roomed with two young girls who went to work in the mornings . . . and they had the kindness never to reproach me. I'd come back with a bottle of Cointreau as an apology, and I'd finish it myself before leaving the next night.

I liked Cointreau a lot. It was in fashion at the time. Twenty years later, in America, there was Drambuie, a whisky liqueur, but it wasn't as good. Paris was a marvel. There were real crowds at the entries and exits of the theaters. People arriving and people leaving. It was lively and people were recovering from the war; they were happy. The nightmare was over, so there was this atmosphere of relief.

LA: And you, what did you want to do with your life, at the time?

EA: I didn't do anything. I hardly touched my doctorate; I didn't write one line. Nothing. I had a scholarship for three years and I spent my time writing a thesis that wasn't my own. I had met an American girl of Russian background who was writing her thesis on Tolstoy, but her French wasn't good, so she would go research at the national library on the rue de Richelieu, and in the evening, I would put it all into French. I would have her talk to explain her notes to me, and that kept me busy for three years.

LA: So, you did the job for her?

EA: I was very happy because during that time I had two passions: my professor, whom I considered extraordinarily beautiful, Étienne Souriau, and my girlfriend who had a Russian name, Taïs. She was very complicated and very jealous. This was a time when people hid their sexuality, but me, I had no clue you were supposed to hide it. I didn't even know what I was thinking, and I remember she was obsessed because before, in America, she had lived with a girlfriend and one of them had been put in jail. It was very hard, people insulted them in the street, in cafés. There was an unbearable ostracism. I had no idea of the persecution endured by homosexual men and women. Many young people in America committed suicide. There were many suicides because they were afraid of their moms finding out. And there was active persecution of women. But my girlfriend had lost her job. She had been a schoolteacher before her doctorate. She had suffered agony.

LA: Your affair lasted a long time?

EA: She was unbearable: "Don't come back, don't go out, don't look at me." It was terrible. And on top of it I was really in love with both of them at the same time. It's very bizarre—that is, I was spellbound by these two people.

LA: One, the man, was your professor.

EA: It was easier, I mean, so to speak; it was against morality. Firstly, we had to see each other at his place, because at mine it was not easy. It was really complicated. There was an age difference. He was older, but it wasn't only age, he had a very different social life. I was nowhere, he was at home. Whereas the other one lived in the same building as me at the student housing. Secondly, one day at the Sorbonne, I was sitting in the lecture hall and Souriau's wife showed up—it was a public lecture. She saw me and she fell over. And that's when I immediately decided it was over. I was hurting her too much.

LA: And so, in those years, your profession was being in love?

EA: Voilà. I had no subject other than waiting for the evening to talk about Tolstoy. I knew all the Russian names in the universe of Tolstoy. It's not a loss, it was better than my doctorate.

LA: What was your doctorate on?

EA: Aesthetic values and the sacred. It was too huge. Tolstoy was much more accessible and very interesting. You know that Tolstoy was a pacifist. Then one day, the French government sent a captain, Captain Desjardins, as an envoy to Tolstoy, who was a cousin of the Tsar, to ask him to convince the Tsar to sign a military alliance with France against Germany. So, Desjardins was at Tolstoy's house and told him: "You will be invaded by Germany if you don't sign this agreement." Tolstoy said: "If the Germans want to come, let them come. We have a lot of empty space." Desjardins returned to Paris and the newspaper *Le Matin* published the front page with one single phrase: "Tolstoy is mad." They printed that on the front page of the paper! There were endless stories. For instance, he had distributed his assets while still living, and his wife was angry. She told him: "But you're leaving nothing for our children." And he replied: "The day our children inherit, we'll have nothing left. The peasants are going to take everything." He foresaw that it was going to erupt, and the proof: one of his sons died in Morocco, another in Paris. All over the world. He had many crying children ... Captain Desjardins actually gave an interview about his trip where he described it: "The children wailed and Tolstoy said: 'It's all very well, it will teach them to suffer later on.'" He let them howl.

LA: Was it you who submitted the thesis or was it your girlfriend?

EA: No, it was her. She got first-class honors. There was the professor Jean-Marie Carré, a famous man in Paris, professor of comparative literature. He congratulated her. There was a page of acknowledgements, all the names were there except for mine ... she hadn't dared, which proves the extent to which she was consumed by fear.

LA: And then? After the defense of the thesis, what did you do? Did you return to work on your own? Did you never finish it?

EA: No, my scholarship was over. I left very quickly for America. And I dropped any idea of studying.

10.

LA: We're going to talk about heat. You were born into heat. Have you always lived in the heat, Etel?

EA: Yes, I loved the heat. In a town like Beirut, it gets so hot in the summer the sheets you're sleeping in are soaked. And when you're young, you can deal with the heat. Now I can't handle it anymore.

LA: But we might say that your painting works with heat, the vibration of pure air?

EA: Yes, my painting isn't cold, that's for sure. I was raised with the notion that there were hot countries and cold countries. And that in the hot countries, people had a corresponding character, same for the cold ones. I was on the hot side.

LA: What is your character?

EA: In hot countries, people are lazy and demanding, yes, a little bit lazy, a little untidy. And certainly not democratic.

LA: How many times in your life have you fallen in love?

EA: Love is a form of heat, really. We don't know what it is. It's a state of grace. Why? Sometimes it's very irrational. And why does a person's presence produce a state of grace that becomes a need? It has a lot to do with the imagination.

LA: And how did you go from love for your professor to love for your girlfriend? How did you switch sexes in the definition of love?

EA: I don't know. It was simultaneous and there was no struggle. There's a mythological component of love. It's the sum of many things which gives the illusion that a person matches all of this. But it's very undefinable. You don't feel, you don't really under-stand. As I've said, love produces its own needs. The person who seems to possess the key to this magic becomes necessary.

LA: Today, you don't know what love is?

EA: Not really. It's a state of absolute well-being. It remains a mys-tery. In any case, it's almost painful, too. It's not . . . I think we don't know. I don't really know.

LA: Is love a state or a condition?

EA: It's a state. We don't know, really.

LA: We say "great love"; have you known a great love?

EA: Great, yes. That is, a sort of obsession that swallows everything; like I said, it's almost painful. It takes up lots of room. It takes up all the room.

LA: Were you stigmatized when you were young because you liked girls? Were you blamed for your homosexuality?

EA: No, no.

LA: You were never bothered?

EA: No. In fact, you're so inside of it that you don't notice. It becomes a requirement. It's a feeling you can't rebuke. You don't know where it comes from. I don't know where it comes from. But there's not only love for a person. One can be possessed by an idea, an idea of poetry. For example, when you read the poems of certain mystics. They truly love God—what do they mean by that? I don't know, but it is love.

LA: What have you loved the most in the world?

EA: At one time, I loved painting, and it was very involved with the mountain. I think I have truly loved the world. The fact that the world exists. One could call it the universe, the world. And the world is closer to the idea of painting because it's physical—it's the world, it's mountains, rivers . . . the world. You can truly love the world. Yes, not always a person. It's the fact of being alive. The feeling of life is an endearing thing.

LA: Do you love being alive?

EA: In general, it's been alright, yes.

LA: You've never wanted to kill yourself?

EA: Rarely. When someone makes me really angry. It's rare, but
. . . suicide comes from fear, it has a lot to do with fear.

LA: But you're not afraid, you're not a fearful person, I think?

EA: Fear is inside of us. It's a structural emotion. We don't know
where it comes from. Fear is awful. It comes from experience.

LA: What are you afraid of?

EA: You're afraid . . . of what you hear, of what you see. You're afraid
to be too dependent. You're afraid . . . human beings are frightened.

LA: And right now, are you afraid?

EA: Right now? Necessarily, because like everyone I think about
how something is ending, and it's got to end as easily as possible.
It's very human. One can also be fearful, not necessarily for oneself, not only for oneself. For example, the Lebanese people are
having a hard time. The world is having a hard time. It leaves a
very bitter taste. This business of the virus is not nice, it's hard,
like a widespread death; it's not easy. And you want it to end, it
seems like it's endless. For example, I've always hated cemeteries.

I've always avoided cemeteries, hospitals, and there's the feeling with this pandemic that it leaves a bitter taste, and it's unpleasant.

LA: But at the same time, you're not afraid of the virus since you haven't been vaccinated?

EA: No, I'm not afraid of the virus, I didn't want to . . . I thought, I'll slip through the net. And we'll see. I didn't want to. But then, it's not always reasonable. I don't want to be reasonable; I want to believe in a little bit of magic, that it will work out, and there you go.

LA: And you like the idea of getting old?

EA: I haven't thought about it much, really not much. I've always been more or less busy.

LA: That's because you're young. Are you still the same person?

EA: There's a continuity. And a carefreeness . . . . You're alive, you continue to be. That's all.

LA: That's already a lot, to be alive?

EA: It's already a lot. You're distracted. Distraction is a state, you're distracted. Fortunately, too.

LA: But is it difficult to be alive all the time?

EA: Yes, it's difficult. We don't know, as I've often said. We live in approximation. Luckily.

LA: So, what are these two paintings I just noticed as I arrived at your place, Etel?

EA: Every morning recently, I get up and, not immediately, but around 11:00 a.m., I go into my studio, and I make one or two paintings. Every day. As far as I can tell, every day it's the same. I don't move things to arrange them in any special way, and there are always bottles lying around, ink bottles or water bottles or others. I've always fancied the bottle as an object. Sometimes I have a hard time throwing one away; it's so beautiful and we throw it out. And there you go, on the floor in my office there are forty or so paintings. We should go look at them.

LA: That's crazy. Every morning?

EA: Every morning I've done one or two, quickly. And my day is done. It starts like that, and I don't want or have the energy to do anything else.

LA: But even so, the morning is like a sort of aesthetic or moral obligation?

EA: Yes, it helps me to confront the day. I can sit now and make a painting. I did one this morning because Simone went to see some sculptors who are going to a quarry where they pick out granite. It's an hour from Erquy. She's going to sleep there and return tomorrow.

That's why she asked her assistant to be here today and tomorrow. Her name is Valentina, she worked in a good gallery in Milan, and she left to come back to Paris with her boyfriend. Simone hired her half time. She's very cheerful. She comes from Puglia.

LA: Every morning you paint, or you draw. And do you write?

EA: No, I haven't written in a long time.

LA: But why don't you write anymore?

EA: It tires me out much more than drawing. I like to draw. The impact of this ink on this white surface attracts me. It makes me want to keep going. Words have too much behind them, and it's tiring in the long run. The line is so immediate. There's a magic, and I have Japanese ink pots that are like little knights. I like the ink a lot. It's beautiful. The blotting effect is beautiful. When you put the ink to the paper, you think the paper is alive and that it's eating the ink. It has absorbed it. Ink is very beautiful. Very, very beautiful. And the fluidity . . .

LA: You choose your paper carefully, too, not only your inks?

EA: I love paper, especially in France with the Arches paper mills. There's an extraordinary paper tradition. The Japanese make paper with rice. It's also very beautiful. The rue du Pont-Louis-Philippe is a paper paradise. All these stores have drawers full, and it's dazzling. I believe paper contributes to the work; you must take great care. It's living, it's beautiful. Paper is beautiful.

LA: Do you touch the paper before drawing?

EA: There's already a layer of gesso on the linen, and the linen is beautiful, it's a lovely material. So, I don't touch it, I draw. When I'm drawing tapestries, then I have to touch the paper. And I really like the contact with the paper. It's cotton, it's wood. Come, come see! You're in for a shock.

LA: Ah yes, I'm flabbergasted. Can you describe it? It's completely new for you, all this.

EA: So, it's very simple. There are two pomegranates. This is the pomegranate. This is a mushroom that Simone made to go with it.

LA: That's some kind of a recycled yogurt bottle.

EA: Right. And that's an old, dried out pomegranate. And those are dried flowers.

LA: So, you thought of this during the night, or it comes like that, right away, in the morning?

EA: It just comes, I don't think about it. Where is the ink? There's the stopper. I don't see the ink, but I see the stopper. This one comes from the Japanese lady's store.

LA: And then over there, right next to your worktable, is the other worktable?

EA: It's supposed to be for writing, and this one for painting.

LA: There's something akin to Henri Matisse in what you're doing right now. The flowerpots, the birds.

EA: Let's paint the ink bottle, then. There. There's a pleasure in it. A single line.

LA: The hand doesn't tremble, and it executes with a single line. In fact, you look at first; but after, you don't look at all anymore.

EA: Right. Here, this goes there.

LA: It's the stopper for the ink bottle.

EA: So here there's this, I'll put it there. You have to keep going. This is the pomegranate, so I'll put it there because I have room. And there, it's done.

LA: You find room in the space of the painting . . .

EA: You see, the contrast is very beautiful, black on this white.

LA: There are several objects you've drawn?

EA: That's the tube of paint. And then voilà, the painting is done.

LA: Look at that.

EA: You also have to want to do it. This, for instance: it's very beautiful. And you decide to reinforce it or not. You don't know why. That one is a bit thinner, but there are daintier pomegranates.

LA: So, there, you're fleshing out the pomegranate . . .

EA: Suggesting a bit, and there you go.

LA: You've done at least three paintings today?

EA: This pomegranate is in almost every painting. And this, see how nice it is to look at. If you go up the street to the left, at the corner, there are these bottles in a shop, you see them from the street. And it's a beautiful ink. It shines.

LA: So, you'll wait until tomorrow now.

EA: Yes, like I'm telling you, you have to trust.

LA: Is the trust a trust in your hand?

EA: Yes, it's in yourself. The more you work, the more you're accustomed. The further you go, the more you break free. Besides, I decide on the paint. And then voilà! There's an immediacy, there's the space. You fill it. You decide to represent what you see, and that's not necessarily reality. It's yours!

LA: But I see that on the worktable there are quite a few paint colors. There's a lot of yellow, lots of tubes of yellow paint.

EA: Yes, those are for paintings I was doing before I began this series in black.

LA: Is that to say you've abandoned color?

EA: No, no, no, but there is such a force in this contrast that color weakens the painting. You see, black and white is so strong that color doesn't add anything, it's not necessary in this case.

LA: I see, on the floor and in front of us, many paintings only in ink, in black and white, no colors. As if it were a new cycle of paintings, then? You've never done that, except in calligraphy, quite some time ago. Is this a return to a form of pictorial calligraphy?

EA: No, I don't think so. It's something else, still. In fact, it's really drawing. The drawing exists and you realize that the drawing is within the object. The drawing guides you and says to you "I am here." Actually, you follow what the object tells you.

LA: Is there something philosophical in this approach? Because I'm thinking of the theories of Merleau-Ponty. How can we take things as themselves? How to capture things themselves?

EA: Well, we do it. For instance, if you don't want to play along, if someone refuses to see a pomegranate in there, there's nothing you can do. But it's there, the pomegranate. I like pomegranates because they're very beautiful. The tree is beautiful, and the fruits are like Christmas ornaments in the tree. We have superstitions in the Greek world, where the pomegranate exists, and the Persians—the Iranians—say it originates in their country. But for the Greeks, the pomegranate is a bit like the horn of plenty, it's full of life, and the juice is very good. You put one or two spoonfuls in a stew and everything is changed. Ah yes! Put pomegranate juice in a salad or on meat. It's very good.

LA: In the other paintings, over there, there are lots of flowers, lots of bouquets of flowers; I told you it still makes me think of a period of Matisse.

EA: Yes, because flowers are inspiring. I can put some flowers here. I love flowers, look, how beautiful. I think I love roses, but I also love jasmine for its scent. I love flowers! But they're poisonous too, sometimes they're not a sure thing.

So here it is, the morning, I wake up, I dab and smudge, and the day is done.

LA: When you're not smudging, you're splashing, is that it? You like to smudge and splash?

EA: Yes, and see the power of this barely visible line. It widens the pomegranate, but by suggestion. I'm not going to darken it.

LA: It should be said that you have drawn the slightly more rounded contour of the pomegranate with a very, very fine line. But you don't wish to make it larger or thicker.

EA: And look, that gives it depth. The eye participates, but there must be this trust. You mustn't hesitate during the work, you must go straight in.

LA: It's funny you say that, because you began painting when your art professor asked: "Can you paint?" And you replied: "No. My mother thinks I'll never learn to paint."

EA: Right, that I was clumsy, and the professor told me: "You believed her?" And her answer changed the world.

LA: And why did your mother say that to you, do you know now?

EA: Because she was very nervous, and it was easier for her to do things herself than to wait for others to do them. With her, it was "Don't touch, don't mess it up, don't get it dirty." We were her guests; we were in her home.

LA: Nothing was yours?

EA: No, nothing.

LA: Not even the space?

EA: No, no, especially not.

LA: You're not angry with your mother now?

EA: It's far back . . .

LA: Yes, it's far. But I mean, in the living room, in your home, there's a photo of your father. But there are no photos of your mother.

EA: No. I haven't thought about it.

So, right, I wake up in the morning and I do one or two things. I don't know where the fatigue comes from. I don't move, I don't do anything, I don't go out, I don't lie down, I sleep sitting up. If I lie down, I choke, I can't breathe. So, I sleep between these two chairs. It's tiring, I'm tired.

LA: When did old age begin?

EA: Oh! It's sneaky, we don't know how it begins. There's not one moment. It's up and down. I really don't know.

LA: But do you like getting old?

EA: I don't think about it. It's been a long time now. Old age has a lot to do with fatigue. It comes on like fatigue. And what is fatigue? It's a lack of momentum. You feel like you're carrying a physical weight. It's physical. It's a comparison; it has to do with memory. The memory of better states. It's a state. I don't know what it is.

LA: This state, do you suffer it or accept it?

EA: You suffer it; you accept it because you can't not.

LA: Do you think this is a very propitious period for you, the last part of your life?

EA: Yes. It's a contradiction, but it's true for many things. Even from the point of view of general thinking, I think better. I don't understand why. You might say I was repressed, that I didn't dare to think to the end or even take a risk with painting. Perspectives change and even boldness. I'm at a moment when the barriers had to break. I don't know any longer.

LA: And that means what, to take risks in painting?

EA: Yes, you take risks. You change. You believe that you've grown at one time, whereas you are growing constantly in one way or another. We call that . . . change.

LA: What changes, according to you? What has changed within you?

EA: What changes? I have to think. The importance I give to certain things, that's what has changed. I think you don't know . . . what you consider to be "having fun."

LA: You would have liked to have had more fun? But you had a lot of fun in your life, Etel.

EA: I don't know if I had a lot of fun. I kept myself very busy.

LA: Did you work too much?

EA: Yes, it's not the same. Have fun! You must have a lot of fun. We don't really enjoy ourselves.

LA: When you paint every morning, you're enjoying yourself anyway, no?

EA: Yeah, I don't know. I've been preoccupied . . .

LA: Preoccupied by the war, a lot?

EA: Yes, there have been wars. We ought to have told ourselves that wars are an absurdity that must be allowed to pass. War is an absurdity.

LA: And we cannot say, alas, that today your country is at peace.

EA: Yes, but there are so many factors. I don't know what the problem is; these are circumstances that must be allowed to pass.

We were speaking of war. War satisfies the illusion that we can resolve problems by emptying out. That we can clear out, sweep away, throw out; and it's probably a necessary illusion. We don't know if everything that exists had to exist. It's a question. Are things thus because they couldn't not have been, couldn't not be?

LA: But human beings also could have not existed. Does this mean that you're referring to the hypothesis of the origin of the world?

EA: Yes, to create a mirror to see better.

LA: To see what better?

EA: What you see.

LA: But what do you see?

EA: What do you see? You're back at the notion that we're full of illusions. Do we see? Do we think we can see? And this is anguish. Anguish is the questioning of sight. Do you really see? What do you call seeing? Can we get rid of something we cannot see? I don't know. But it has a lot to do with it . . . and painting fixes in place. Painting is an assertion; you assert something when you paint. It's interesting. This assertion must supplant other assertions.

11.

LA: When you paint, you're describing the world that you see, but you're also asserting your existence, since it's you who is painting?

EA: Yes, you have this need for assertion. Because what we call creation is to produce an assertion. This is what it is to create, and it's extraordinary, this notion of making a reality appear. Even if it means admitting that the meaning of this reality escapes you as you create it. And why not? When we say God created the world . . . has he detached himself from it? And we invoke this God, we solicit him nonstop. Maybe he's turned the page, once and for all.

LA: He's left us all alone. But you've told me you don't believe in God.

EA: In the sense I just gave you, he has very likely moved on for good, I don't know.

LA: God is dead, as Nietzsche says. But perhaps the gods aren't dead themselves?

EA: No, but there's the temptation to say that if God is dead, everything is dead. That is what Nietzsche actually says, and that's so, so terrible. It goes against our instinct, our need for life. One might also say that God has freed us by dying. It's interesting. Me, I think that God has freed us and that we're splashing around. You see, we're swimming. We go forward, we go back. We're asking questions.

LA: We haven't actually grown, then? It's funny, Etel, you've used the word "splashing" several times. To splash around, it's like what children do in puddles when they're little?

EA: Yes, they splash. You make do. It's like fatigue. Are you subjected to it? You wade through it . . .

LA: Is fatigue an enemy or an accomplice?

EA: When you're wading through, you're continually changing perspective. That's what it is. Sometimes you see one thing, sometimes another, and it carries you away. You cannot die several times. You are there and you move forward, it's true.

LA: Would you like to die multiple times?

EA: In a certain way, we have . . . we have died several times. But each time we've woken up. I have heart problems. It complicates lots of things. I can't go to concerts anymore, since my standing up in the middle would disturb everyone else. Even long train trips are becoming difficult. I've also got someone who spends the night here. All this is tiring. You have to adjust your life to your problems.

LA: I'd like for us to talk about happiness. Ah, that makes you smile.

EA: Happiness, it arises. There are moments of happiness that arise of themselves. It's good, fortunately.

LA: And your last moment of happiness, what was it?

EA: It's simple. Lunch at midday, it's a little rest.

LA: And then the light today is very beautiful. The sun is back. Are you a feminist?

EA: I'm a feminist. Well, yes. There's every reason to be. It's a constant battle.

LA: When have you been a feminist? When did feminism begin for you?

EA: It began in America. A professor colleague of mine asked what my salary was. When I told her, she said, "But this is unacceptable, go ask for a raise immediately." I was bothered; I hate asking for things. She told me: "If you come back to lunch with me and you haven't asked for a raise, I won't speak to you." So, I went to see the president of the college, and after a half hour she asked me why I'd come, and I replied: "To tell you hello." She gave me a hug, and I thought: I'll write her a note instead. Which I did, and I immediately got a significant raise. And I wondered: Why was I automatically paid less? And it's all like that.

Yes, I'm really a feminist because we have such a tough time. For example, I had a relationship that didn't interest me all that much, but anyway . . . with a guy who was married and had no kids. And he didn't know if it was because of him or his wife. And it's hard to say, because voilà, I got "caught." I had, as they say, "fallen" pregnant. And his reaction was: "Well, now I know it wasn't because of me." That's what he said; whereas I was devastated, this guy was very pleased with himself because he knew he wasn't sterile.

LA: What did you do with the child you were expecting? Did you have an abortion?

EA: I had to be rid of it.

LA: How awful! Because it was very difficult and very dangerous.

EA: It wasn't easy because it wasn't a thing to take lightly.

LA: Never, I think.

EA: I remember when there was the uprising that Delphine Seyrig participated in. She minimized the problem, but it's not an easy thing. You're getting rid of a living thing. So, I was in total dismay, and I even felt contempt for the guy. I was like his guinea pig. It was a cruel thing.

LA: But today, you think that women's rights are better respected since the women's movement? Did you participate in the first women's struggles in the United States, Etel?

EA: You know, it's very difficult to resist power, and even the women's movement had this problem. My only novel was published by Editions Des Femmes, so I knew them. And Antoinette Fouque was admirable because she'd been in a wheelchair her whole life. But she had a very acute power problem. And that divided these women amongst themselves.

LA: It was the "Psych and Po" movement, Psychoanalysis and Politics, and Antoinette ruled like a queen.

EA: Antoinette . . . power went to her head.

LA: And in contemporary art, do you think women painters are pushed aside and paid less than men?

EA: They've had to bargain with gallerists, and they've had much more trouble to gain real acceptance.

LA: And to be recognized on the market?

EA: Besides, even today, there are women who are still in the shadow of a man. For example, Sonia Delaunay is still the wife of Robert Delaunay . . .

LA: It continues to this day, then, the inferiorizing of women? And the #MeToo movement, what do you think of that? How do you see the future of women?

EA: It's a problem because there are some who abuse it more than they should, and it's traumatizing for men, too. Where does harassment begin? I don't know.

LA: But you find there has been an evolution for the status of women since your youth?

EA: They've fought for it. There's a radical change.

LA: No one tried to marry you off to a man? Your parents or your family?

EA: Yes, I mean, with my mother it was: "Get married! That way I can die in peace, there's someone who will ensure you have a house." There were problems of authority. She was held responsible for everything that happened to me. If a girl spent the night out, she could be murdered when she came home. They called it an "honor killing."

LA: You witnessed things this atrocious?

EA: I didn't see them, but I knew a woman who came to the house, and her young son had "needed" to kill his sister because she had spent the night out. And I had written a short piece on this story, which I called "An Honor Killing." I know how hard it was because the mother had a daughter murdered and a young son who wound up in prison.

And at the office, a true story: there was a young man, and my colleagues warned me: "Watch out! He killed his sister." He hadn't wanted to do it; his family had forced him to say he had done it because his older brother had started a small political party, and since the younger boy would serve less time in prison due to his age, he had been forced to take the blame to protect his brother's career. It was very hard because people avoided him and called him a criminal. And he was kind, he was in love with me, and I caused him problems without meaning to. My mother took my money, I had to give her the money I earned. I was attending Catholic boarding school for the baccalaureate. And my teacher, whom I liked a lot, was favoring . . . actually the entire convent favored this one student, because her family had orchards; they were very rich people and they sent cases of tangerines. Her name was Yvonne, and she was the cousin of Simone's brother-in-law. I learned that later. I couldn't stand it; I was furious and thought: Everyone sucks up to Yvonne because her parents send tangerines. So, I decided to make a large gift to the nun. I bought her a watch, and the poor nun said to me: "But Etel, I need permission from the mother superior . . . ," which she obtained. And then my mother went to get money and it was missing. So, she says: "You're the only one who's been in that room, where is the money?" I told her someone borrowed it from me, I said it was the young man from the office who asked to borrow money. She saw whom I was referring to, and she'd heard that he killed his own sister, on top of everything. She went to the office, screaming, upbraiding him. I begged him to say he borrowed the money. Because my mother could be violent, and she would have gone to the nun to take back the watch. I would have lost face. The poor boy endured my mother's yelling in front of the other employees. He was humiliated twice. He was crying and saying: "I didn't kill my sister."

I don't have a single copy of this piece, "An Honor Killing," but it was published by Éditions de L'Arche. I should go by and get one. They read it in a high school somewhere and the students asked me: "But why didn't they run away together?" I replied: "But do you realize? They had nothing to eat, they had no money. They had nowhere to go." There are still honor killings . . .

LA: Still to this day in Lebanon?

EA: In Jordan, sometimes. In Pakistan, certainly. And among the Greeks, it existed, but it was less common.

LA: Would you have liked to have children?

EA: Not really. I didn't think much about it.

LA: Have you suffered much during your life?

EA: Yes, and . . . I saw . . . it's a problem. It's unresolvable because after an experience like abortion, women have problems. They're frightened, and men don't understand. They call them "frigid." And what might that do to you? They don't understand what women go through. Many women in the Muslim world have committed suicide because of such things. Men don't understand that they go nights without sleeping. Women have specific problems and they're embarrassed. It's not talked about.

LA: Woman artist or simply artist? Do you believe in God now?

EA: I don't know what that means. I don't think so. I don't know. No, it's very abstract. I believe there are certainly things we don't know and don't understand. We're not the last word, that's all. And it doesn't go beyond that, but I believe in a universe that brings us together, as much as we are part of it. I believe anyway that we have, all human beings, things in common. And that's important.

LA: In fact, it's upon waking that you create, and you paint, so is there a link with sleep?

EA: It has nothing to do with real sleep, no. Last night I saw a person who has been very important to me come to tell me goodbye in a dream, crossing as if in center stage at the theater from one end to the other, to the ending. That, I saw.

LA: And was it someone who died afterward, who came to tell you goodbye in the dream?

EA: She came to tell me "I'm leaving." One time. And it was true. I've seen very beautiful countryside, especially rivers. I've seen a lot of water in my dreams . . . and I swim. And then, enormous rivers that flow together. I've seen that in dreams, but it doesn't last; I forget after a day or two. My mother had a book, a dictionary of dreams in Greek; for example, if you saw a lion, if the lion bit you, it's a bad sign. I remember the lion because there was a photo of him, and my mother was very superstitious. There were lucky days and unlucky days of the year. The unlucky days of the year were days when you shouldn't buy land or shouldn't go on a trip. She believed in this business of lucky and unlucky days, in the interpretation of dreams, but she read novels too. For example, she read the *Life of Cleopatra* maybe ten times, because Cleopatra was so mean. She put her boyfriends to death. So, you couldn't get close to her, or you'd end up dead. And she defied Anthony and Caesar, she spoke patronizingly to them. But my mother read the saints as well, the lives of the saints. It was a naive belief. It was quite touching, besides, because she spoke to the Holy Virgin as if to a friend. It was a conversation between women; she came to tell her about her problems.

But today it's Spring. There's this beautiful light. Look—the flowers in the vase. The olive tree on the balcony. It's a good day.

TRANSLATOR'S ACKNOWLEDGMENTS

Huge thanks to Flora Iff-Noël and Lindsay Turner for their perspicacity and generosity; to Gia Gonzales, Lindsey Boldt, Lina Bergamini, Santiago Valencia, and Kit Schluter for their attention, their patience, persistence, insight and indulgence; and to Stephen Motika, a special gratitude for his wisdom, zest and care, which help to clarify the meetness of things.

ETEL ADNAN was born in Beirut, Lebanon in 1925. She studied philosophy at the Sorbonne, U.C. Berkeley, and at Harvard, and taught at Dominican College in San Rafael, California, from 1958 to 1972. In solidarity with the Algerian War of Independence (1954–1962), Adnan began to resist the political implications of writing in French and became a painter. Then, through her participation in the movement against the Vietnam War (1959–1975), she began to write poetry and became, in her words, "an American poet." In 1972, she returned to Beirut and worked as cultural editor for two daily newspapers—first for *Al Safa*, then for *L'Orient le Jour*. Her novel *Sitt Marie-Rose*, published in Paris in 1977, won the France-Pays Arabes award and has been translated into more than ten languages. In 1977, Adnan re-established herself in California, making Sausalito her home, with frequent stays in Paris. Adnan is the author of more than a dozen books in English, including *Journey to Mount Tamalpais* (1986), *The Arab Apocalypse* (1989), *In the Heart of the Heart of Another Country* (2005), and *Sea and Fog* (2012), winner of the Lambda Literary Award for Lesbian Poetry and the California Book Award for Poetry. Her book *Time*, translated by Sarah Riggs, received the Griffin Poetry Prize in 2020. In 2014, she was awarded one of France's highest cultural honors: l'Ordre de Chevalier des Arts et Lettres. Her paintings have been widely exhibited, including Documenta 13, the 2014 Whitney Biennial, CCA Wattis Institute for Contemporary Arts, The New Museum, and Museum der Moderne Salzburg. In 2021, the Guggenheim Museum in New York presented an exhibition of her work. She died in November 2021.

LAURE ADLER was born in 1950. She has written several books on the history of women, and a prizewinning biography of Marguerite Duras. She has worked in publishing and as the Director of the France Culture radio station. She now works as a journalist and broadcaster.

ETHAN MITCHELL (b. 1977) is an editor and translator living in Berkeley, CA.

NIGHTBOAT BOOKS

Nightboat Books, a nonprofit organization, seeks to develop audiences for writers whose work resists convention and transcends boundaries. We publish books rich with poignancy, intelligence, and risk. Please visit nightboat. org to learn about our titles and how you can support our future publications.

The following individuals have supported the publication of this book. We thank them for their generosity and commitment to the mission of Nightboat Books:

Kazim Ali, Anonymous (8), Mary Armantrout, Jean C. Ballantyne, Thomas Ballantyne, Bill Bruns, John Cappetta, V. Shannon Clyne, Ulla Dydo Charitable Fund, Photios Giovanis, Amanda Greenberger, Vandana Khanna, Isaac Klausner, Shari Leinwand, Anne Marie Macari, Elizabeth Madans, Martha Melvoin, Caren Motika, Elizabeth Motika, The Leslie Scalapino - O Books Fund, Robin Shanus, Thomas Shardlow, Rebecca Shea, Ira Silverberg, Benjamin Taylor, David Wall, Jerrie Whitfield & Richard Motika, Arden Wohl, Issam Zineh

This book is made possible, in part, by grants from the New York City Department of Cultural Affairs in partnership with the City Council and the New York State Council on the Arts Literature Program.